SELECTED
HIGHLAND FOLK TALES

Selected

HIGHLAND FOLKTALES

R Macdonald Robertson

David St John Thomas Publisher

Cover photograph:
Black Mount, Rannoch Moor,
courtesy Colin Baxter Photography Ltd
Unit 2/3, Block 6, Caldwellside Industrial Estate,
Lanark ML11 6SR.

British Library Cataloguing in Publication Data

Robertson, Ronald Macdonald
Selected Highland Folktales.
– New ed
I. Title
398.209411
ISBN 0-946537-79-8

First published by Oliver & Boyd 1961
Republished by David & Charles 1977
This paperback edition published 1993

Printed in Great Britain
by The Redwood Press, Melksham
for David St John Thomas Publisher
PO Box 4, Nairn IV12 4HU

Dedicated

The Royal Celtic Society

My sincere thanks are due to the Royal Celtic Society and to my many Highland and Island friends who by their kind co-operation have made this book possible.

R.M.R.

Preface

"Tradition is a meteor which, once it falls,
cannot be rekindled."

A belief in the supernatural prevails almost universally among
the tribes of mankind. Man has always chafed at the limitations
of his knowledge, and has tended to see in any unusual
experience the manifestation of mysterious powers. The
Scottish Highlands are a perfect setting for contacts of all
kinds with the supernormal. John Buchan writes in " Mid-
winter " about the North of Scotland:—" It is the land of the
edge of moorlands and the ruins of forests and the twilight
before dawn, and strange knowledge dwells in it."

The depth of the solitude, the huge peaks, the deep chasms
between the rocks, the dark gloom of the forests, the deep
black loch—are full of associations of awe, grandeur and
mystery. There is hardly a glen or river north of the Forth
that does not possess its own supernatural inhabitant.

In spite of the advent of so-called civilization, the old
beliefs linger on among the silent fastnesses of the hills. From
clachan and shieling come tales, marvellous tales of phantasms
of the living and apparitions of the dead, of compacts with the
devil and fights with the same dark being; of fairies who haunt
green knolls and grey cliffs; of mermaids and witches, and
strange incredible monsters in loch and river and sea, as well as
dwellers in the sky.

It is in the belief that every story of the supernormal is of
value as a factor in the spiritual development of the human mind
that these pages are presented, and most of these legends have
been gleaned from places which possessed a charming old-time
atmosphere, in an alluring land of wilderness and wonder,

where occasional wreaths of blue peat-smoke curl skywards from the clachans. Long may this old-time atmosphere be respected and preserved.

Important

Any similarity between the stories in this volume and those contained in other published collections is due to the fact that many of the tales are traditional.

The material for the legends has been derived mainly from oral sources, and books have been avoided as authorities.

The reader is free to draw his own inferences from the tales; with regard to responsibility for their accuracy, the writer can only say—

" Ma's breug bh' uam e, is breug dhomh e "
(If it be a lie as told by me, it was a lie as told to me).

R.M.R.

Edinburgh, 1961

New Introduction

RONALD MACDONALD ROBERTSON was one of several memorable and well liked personalities who were out and about in Edinburgh in the nineteen-forties and fifties. He was a friendly and convivial man, distinguished by several immediately apparent characteristics. He almost always wore Highland dress, with a kilt in the tartan of the Robertsons of Strathardle in Perthshire. In addressing friends and acquaintances he employed a form of speech which combined the etiquette of the courtroom with the courtesy and personal concern more typical of a bygone age.

Whenever encountered, usually in one of the streets of Edinburgh's Old Town, close to the Courts, the libraries and the newspaper offices, he was invariably brimming over with enthusiasm for some newly explored topic of Scottish clan or folklore interest. With this he would regale any companion, despite the east wind, snow showers, or the noise of passing traffic, for at least the next several minutes. He was never a man to meet when hurrying to catch a train.

R. Macdonald Robertson was the son of a doctor. He went to Edinburgh Academy, studied law and became a Writer to the Signet in 1925. Concurrent with his legal career he exercised a passion for the remote north-west Highlands, persistently wandering in that vast wilderness with a knapsack and fishing rod, and collecting the stories of the local people as he encountered them. The resulting books—*In Scotland with a Fishing Rod*, *Angling in Wildest Scotland* and *Wade the River, Drift the Loch*— were best-sellers in their own sphere.

Meanwhile he was secretary to the Scottish Clan Societies, and wrote on clan and folklore matters for *Scotland's Magazine* and for an Edinburgh evening newspaper.

It was early in the 1950's that I was invited to his home—named "Straloch" after the seat of the Robertson chiefs in Strathardle—in the Comely Bank district of Edinburgh. In the attic I was confronted with the awesome sight of a large tin trunk crammed to its lid with pages of manuscript and typescript—the result of years of note-taking, holiday jotting and recorded conversations, all either still in handwriting or typed in single spacing on both sides of the paper! The work of sorting, piecing together and editing this mass of material called for some of the irrepressible enthusiasm of Macdonald Robertson himself, but the resulting book's many readers around the world found the effort well worth while.

Macdonald Robertson was the first to concede that the tales he collected direct from the crofter fishermen of Sutherland and country folk elsewhere were not to be regarded as a serious scholarly contribution to Scottish lore and legend, but as entertainment of the kind traditional in these remote regions, where the story-teller has always enjoyed an especially high regard.

"If it was true as told to me, then it is true as I am telling it to you," Macdonald Robertson was fond of quoting with a twinkle, and he was content to leave it at that.

R. Macdonald Robertson died in 1968 at the age of sixty-nine. A wayside seat near his home in Comely Bank is inscribed: "Presented by the Clans and Highland Associations in memory of Ronald Macdonald Robertson, W.S., F.S.A. (Scot.) Angler and author. 1968."

On being informed of the proposed reprinting of *Selected Highland Folktales* in the year of the Gathering of the Clans in Edinburgh, I was pleased but not surprised. More than anything, the project has evoked the stocky, kilted figure rounding an Edinburgh street corner, hand outstretched, with the characteristic greeting: "My dear fellow! This is indeed a great pleasure! I have just had word of something I simply must pass on to you!"

Jeremy Bruce-Watt
Edinburgh 1977

Contents

*A complete list of the Tales in each
section can be found on page* 210

Fairy Lore

" ' How will you go back? ' said the woman.
' Nay, that I do not know.'
' Because I have heard, that for those who enter Fairy Land, there is no going back. They must go on, and go through it.' "

1

FAIRIES

Na Sìthichean

In any collection of Highland and Island legends, the first and most important place must be assigned to the Sìth or Fairy People.

Throughout the greater part of the North, the fairies have become people of the past. A common belief is that they existed once, though they are not now to be seen. They were believed to dwell inside green hillocks and knolls, in gorgeous palaces. They usually appeared as men or women of small stature, dressed in green or grey, though they could assume any shape at will.

While the Sìth had no inborn antagonism towards human beings, and were occasionally known to do good turns to their favourites, they were very quick to take offence, capricious in their behaviour, and delighted in playing tricks on their mortal neighbours. These cantrips had to be patiently endured, as resistance or hostility might lead to dreadful reprisals—the kidnapping of children or even adults. An attitude of passive friendliness on the human side was therefore assumed to be eminently desirable. Contact with the fairies was never productive of good in the end.

People deemed it advisable to maintain good relations with the " Secret Commonwealth," and with this end in view, bestowed on them various titles such as " Good Neighbours." Scott refers to this practice in " Rob Roy," when he makes Bailie Nicol Jarvie say to his companion, as they are passing the fairy-hill near the eastern extremity of the valley of Aberfoyle—

" They ca' them . . . Daoine Sìth, quhilk signifies, as I understand, men of peace: meaning thereby to make their gudewill. And we may e'en as well ca' them that too, Mr. Osbaldistone, for there's nae gude in speaking ill o' the laird within his ain bounds."

Cold iron, in the form of a horseshoe, was believed to be the most effective charm against the Sìth, and the cross of rowan fastened above the door of many a Highland homestead was intended to keep the house and its occupants safe from their interference.

Fairy music

Although they often got mortals to play the pipes for them, the " sìth " were reputed to have great musical skill of their own, and when men and women of human race were stolen and taken into their dwellings, one of the greatest inducements to stay was the allurement of the fairy music.

Of Fairy Music, James Stephens writes:—

... from the darkness there came ... a low, sweet sound; thrilling joyous, thrillingly low; so low the ear could scarcely note it, so sweet the ear wished to catch nothing else and would strive to hear it rather than all sounds that may be heard by man: the music of another world! the unearthly dear melody of the 'sìth'! So sweet it was that the sense strained to hear it, and having reached must follow drowsily in its wake, and would merge in it, and could not return to its own place until that strange harmony was finished and the ear restored to freedom.

One story tells how a brother and sister went on a starry night to Kennavarra Hill, to examine a bird snare they had set in a hollow near a stream. As they climbed down into the hollow they heard beautiful music coming from beneath their feet. Terror-stricken, they fled home. This tale was often related by the girl when an old woman.

Near Portree in Skye there is a hillock called " Sìthean Beinne Bhòidhich " (the fairy dwelling of the pretty hill). Those who pass it at night have heard the most beautiful music coming from under the ground; but have been unable to trace the exact spot from which it emanates.

Curious plaintive music, said to be the fairy organ, is frequently heard from under the arches of Fraisgall Cave, in Sutherland; and strange singing blends with the melodies, as if pleading with the listener to come away to the Land Under the Waves where the sea-fairies have their dwelling.

3

Strains of exquisite melody, as if played by a piper marching at the head of a procession, are to be heard going underground from the Harp Hillock to the Dun of Caslais, in Tiree; and many a wayfarer is said to have been lured into the knoll—never to be seen again.

"Cnocan nam Ban" (The Women's Hillock) in Barr Glen, West Kintyre, and "Cnocan na Cainntearachd" (Hillock of Discourse), in the same district, are two fairy hills—famous for music and eloquence.

On the high ground above Kyle Rhea, near the present boundary between Ross-shire and Inverness-shire, stands a cairn of stones known as "Carn Clann Mhic Cruimein" (Cairn of the Clan MacCrimmon), marking the spot where a number of the MacCrimmons of Glen Elg were slaughtered by a band of Mathesons from Loch Alsh. The sweetest fairy music "in all Scotland" is said to have been heard coming from this old cairn.

The fairies of Pennygown

There is a green hillock near the Pennygown township in Mull which was for long believed to be the abode of a company of "wee folk" benevolently disposed towards the human race.

There fairies could apparently turn their hands to any task, and the people of the district were in the habit of leaving overnight by the *sithean* (fairy hill) all sorts of work for them to do—material to be spun or woven, farm implements and domestic utensils to be repaired, torn clothing to be mended, and the like. When the local folk returned next morning they invariably found the task executed to their entire satisfaction.

There happened to be one villager, however, who persisted in leaving them more and still more difficult tasks to undertake. One night he left by their hillock a piece of driftwood which he had picked up on the sea-shore, with instructions that it was to be made into a ship's mast. When the villagers came next morning to collect the property left overnight, they found none of the tasks executed. This last request had angered the fairies so much that they had left their hillock, in disgust, for good.

The dancing fishermen of Iona

Once upon a time in Iona, a fisherman was under the spell of the fairy folk for a whole year and a day.

According to the story, two fishermen were returning from the fishing vessel when they heard spirited music coming from a *brugh* (fairy dwelling), and observed several of the " wee folk " dancing. One of the men joined the dancers without even waiting to lay down his catch of fish; but the other, remembering that a piece of metal acted as a protective charm against fairy spells, prudently stuck a fish hook into the door of the *brugh* before entering. He was thus free to leave when he wished; but his unfortunate companion was forced to remain —and was found by his friend when the year had gone—still dancing!

He was trailed outside the fairy dwelling, still carrying his string of fish. By some strange magical coincidence they had remained fresh all the time he had been in the *brugh;* but now they fell rotten from the string.

The golden bridge of Dornoch

No matter on what work the fairies were engaged, it was always easy to stop them by uttering a blessing. On one occasion at least, this proved very unfortunate.

Across the mouth of the Dornoch Firth there stretches a bar of sand—a source of danger to navigation—which is known locally as " The Gizzen Briggs " (Noisy Bridge) because of the noise made by the tide rushing over it. The hoarse roaring of the Gizzen Briggs, especially during frosty weather, is so loud as to be heard at a distance of many miles, and it is the infallible barometer of the old residents, to whose practised ear its varied intonation is a sure sign of the coming weather.

The story of its origin is that the fairies, tired of crossing from Ross-shire to Sutherland in their cockle-shell boats, began to build a beautiful bridge of gold across the firth. When it was half-way built, a man who was passing, marvelled at the magnificence of the work, lifted his hands and exclaimed, " God bless the workmen! ", whereupon the " little people " jumped into the sea and never returned to their bridge, which soon became covered with sand and shingle—as it appears today. The local people say that the moaning of the Gizzen Briggs is really the lamentation of the fairies ; and that whosoever digs deep enough under the sand will find the golden bridge.

The fairies and the MacCrimmons of Skye

Sometimes the fairies communicate their musical skill to mortal favourites. To them has been ascribed the excellence in music of the MacCrimmons, for centuries pipers to the Macleods.

"An Gille Dubh Macruimein" (the Black Lad MacCrimmon) was the youngest of three sons, and the least thought of by his father. One day, his father and brothers went to a fair, and he was left at home alone. When they had gone, " An Gille Dubh " took down the chanter and began to play on it. He walked out-of-doors as he played, and wandered on till he came to the dwelling of " Beanshith Uaimh an Oir " (the Fairy Woman of the Cave of Gold) which he entered. She handed him a silver chanter on which she gave him a lesson. Then she told him to think of any tune he pleased and play it in the way that she had shown him. He did so, and played the tune skilfully. Then the fairy woman said to The Black Lad, " A nis is tu Rìgh nam Piobairean. Cha robh do leithid romhad, agus cha bhi do leithid as do dheidh " (Now thou art the King of Pipers. Thine equal was not before thee, and thine equal shall not be after thee). So saying, she disappeared.

6

When she had gone, there was not a tune that "An Gille Dubh" could think of which he did not try and which he could not play with ease.

To the teaching of the fairy woman, and to the magic chanter which remained in the family as an heirloom, the MacCrimmons were indebted for their fame as pipers.

The fairies of Findhorn

The banks of the River Findhorn were in olden days believed to be a favourite haunt of the "sith," and the district is rich in legend about them. The place-name Dulsie is an imperfect form of the Gaelic *tulla sith* (Knoll of the Fairies), and the fairy hillock there is still regarded locally as an uncanny place. It was said to be the rendezvous of all the fairies up and down the Findhorn. When General Wade's military road to Fort George was made, the Dulsie ford was superseded by a stone bridge, and since then (1764) it is said that the fairies began to disappear.

The Macqueens of Pollochaig were special favourites of the Findhorn fairies, and possessed a talisman of great virtue in the shape of three magic candles. At one time the beautiful wife of Mackintosh of Daviot was stolen by the fairies, and it was believed that she was kept prisoner in a fairy palace in the heart of the Doune of Daviot.

The wise man of the county—Captain MacGillivray of Dunmaglass—declared that the only way of entering the underground passage leading to the fairy dwelling in the Doune was by the light of the Macqueen's magic candles, and requested the loan of these.

Macqueen was loth to part with the fairies' gift; but his loyalty to his Chief and Lady Mackintosh was so great that at last he gave them up.

The lady was restored to her husband; but when the candles were returned to Macqueen their virtue had left them, and from that time nothing but misfortune befell him and his family.

The old mansion of Pollochaig now stands in ruins; but still bears witness to the truth of the saying that one should " never part with any gift the fairies bestow."

On both sides of the River Findhorn between the heights of Downduff and Duncarn, there are numerous cairns. Unfortunately for antiquarians, a belief that they contained treasure has led to most of them being opened and the stones removed.

A prophecy was made by an old " seer " who declared on his death-bed that:—

Between Carn Cry and Carn Foord
There lies a seven-coupled room of gold.

The cairns between these two points have been ruthlessly explored but no room filled with immense treasure has been discovered.

One of the few cairns still left unopened is the Silver Hillock in the Darnaway Woods—probably because the prophecy mentioned gold, not silver; but it is not unlikely that seekers after treasure-trove may yet investigate its mysteries.

The Spunkies

An' oft your moss-traversing spunkies
Decoy some wight that late and drunk is;
The bleezin, surst, mischievous monkies
Delude his eyes,
Till in some miry slough he sunk is
Ne'er more to rise.
(Burns' Address to the De'il)

Tales of Spunkies are not very common. The Spunkie was an agent, formerly employed by the Enemy of Mankind to accomplish their destruction: And, in all truth, he could not have taken into his pay a servant more faithful to his trust than the spunkie. Whenever the traveller had the misfortune to lose his way, or wherever there was a prospect of deluding him from it, this vigilant " link-boy " was ever at hand, to light him into ill fortune.

The traveller's attention would be arrested by the most resplendent light, apparently reflected from a window not far distant—a light which, however, as the traveller approached, receded from him like the rainbow. Still pursuing his course towards it, the wily spunkie manoeuvred so dexterously that the unhappy wanderer was speedily decoyed towards the nearest moss or precipice.

The fiddlers of Tomnahurich

Long ago, when the only bridge over the River Ness was an old oak one crumbling with age, two fiddlers, Farquhar Grant and Thomas Cumming, came from Strathspey to Inverness in the hope of making some money and played in the streets. They reached Inverness on a winter evening, when snow lay on the ground and the air was keen with frost. They began to play their favourite airs; but few paid any attention to them and none thought of offering any reward.

Despondently, they were making their way as dusk fell towards the river bank, when they saw a solitary figure coming to meet them—an old man with a white beard, wearing a green cloak and a curious red peaked cap. To the surprise of the fiddlers, he addressed them by name, and offered them a large fee if they would come and play for him and his friends.

He led them at a headlong pace across the bridge and over the rough moorland towards the low hill of Tomnahurich, which rises abruptly from the level ground like a great up-turned boat. Half way up the hill, the old man stamped on the ground three times with his right foot. A door opened and the fiddlers followed their guide into a lofty hall, ablaze with lights. All round the walls were tables laden with food and wine; and the room was filled with a gay company of " little people," dressed in green.

After they had eaten and drunk, the fiddlers began to play reels and strathspeys, filling the room with their merry music. Untiringly they played, and as untiringly the company danced, until the little old man reappeared and told the two men that morning had come and the ball was over. He led them to the door on the hill and gave them gold for their services. The

9

men had never seen so much wealth before, and Thomas Cumming in his gratitude cried, " May God bless you and your people ! " As he uttered the name of the Deity, the little old man vanished; and when they looked at where the door had been they saw only the bare hillside.

Marvelling greatly, they made their way to town, to find it changed. Instead of the old oak bridge across the river there was a stone one with seven arches. The buildings were not the same; the people wore clothes of a different pattern, and spoke English. They were laughed at because of the stupid questions they asked; so made their way back to Strathspey. Here they gazed with wonder on the inscriptions on the tombstones in the churchyard. Their own names were there, along with those of friends and contemporaries !

Together they entered the church, just as the minister was pronouncing the benediction. As soon as he uttered the name of God, the two fiddlers crumbled into dust before the eyes of the astonished congregation. The fairy gold they carried fell on the floor as a heap of withered leaves.

It was not one night they had spent in the Fairy Hill of Tomnahurich, but a hundred years !

Duncan Fraser and the fairies

Many years ago, on a farm in a remote part of Sutherland, there was employed a man named Duncan Fraser. One day he was sent by his master to cut peats on a piece of moorland at one end of which was a little hillock known as the Fairy Mound.

The man set to work with a will, and soon had cut quite a number of peats. Suddenly he heard a voice exclaiming, " Put back that turf on the roof of my house at once ! " Looking up in fright, he saw the tiny figure of a woman dressed in green, with long golden hair hanging loosely round her shoulders. Duncan had heard of the " sìth," and knew what harm they could work on mortals who offended them, so he hastened to replace the divots which must have formed the roof of a fairy dwelling. When he looked round, the strange figure had vanished and he hurried homewards to tell the story to his master, and to beg him to have the peats cut from another part of the moor.

The farmer laughed at the tale, declaring that he had no belief in fairies and ordered Duncan to go back at once and lift all the peats. The man did as he was told, in fear and trembling, and was surprised and relieved to find that he was left unmolested.

Months passed, till Autumn came again, and Duncan had almost forgotten the adventure. On the very day on which the peats had been lifted the year before, he left the farm to go to his cottage, carrying with him a can of milk for his wife. His way lay by the Fairy Mound, and when he reached it he felt so tired that he sat down to rest, and soon fell asleep. When he awoke, the moon was shining brightly, and round about him was dancing a band of fairies, singing and laughing. They seized his hands, and soon he found himself dancing and laughing with the elfin crowd. The revelry went on all through the night.

Then came the sound of a cock crowing in the farmyard, and the fairy band rushed towards the mound, dragging Duncan with them. A door opened, shutting again with a bang as soon as the fairies entered. The Little Folk sank down exhausted, and poor bewildered Duncan sat on a piece of rock, wondering what was to happen next. Even when the fairies awoke and began to move about, he still sat on in a kind of daze, making no attempt to get away. At last someone tapped his hand, and he saw in front of him the little woman in the green dress, who a year ago had ordered him to replace the turf.

" Once more," she said, " the grass has grown over my roof. Go home, but swear never to speak of what you have seen here."

Duncan gladly gave his oath of silence, and he was allowed to leave the fairy dwelling. He found his can of milk where he had left it, as he thought, the night before, and set off joyfully for home.

A great surprise awaited him. His children were now well grown, and looked on him as a stranger, while his wife stared as if she saw a ghost. When convinced that he was indeed her husband, she reproached him for deserting her. And then

Duncan knew that he had been in fairyland for seven whole years, while he worked out the punishment laid on him by the " Wee Folk."

Sgeulachd a' choire

There lived near Inverness a farmer's wife who had a large cauldron. Each day a " bean-shìth " (fairy woman) used to come to the farm for the cauldron and without a word seize it to take it away. Each time she did so, the housewife said, " Dleasaidh gobha gual, gu iarunn fuar a bhruich; dleasaidh coire cnàimh 's a chur slàn gu teach " (A smith is entitled to coals, in order to heat cold iron; a cauldron is entitled to bones, and to be sent home whole). This made the fairy-woman bring back the cauldron every night, filled with flesh and bones.

One day the woman was going from home, and told her husband that if he repeated the spell, the cauldron would be returned as usual. Left alone, the farmer was working on his thatching when he saw a slight figure dressed in green approaching him. Sensing that this was the " bean-shìth," he became afraid and went into the house and shut the door. He was so frightened that he did not speak a single word to the fairy-woman.

When she found the door closed, the " bean-shìth " went up on the roof above the smoke-hole, and the cauldron rose to meet her. Night came, but the cauldron did not return. When the farmer's wife came back and saw that it had gone, she blamed her husband, calling him " a dhonainn dhona " (good-for-nothing wretch); and set off for the " cnoc-sìth " (fairy hillock) to reclaim her property.

She found no one inside but a couple of old, grey-haired men, fast asleep. She entered softly without speaking, and picked up the cauldron to take with her; but it was heavy with the remnants of food that were in it, and knocked against the door-post and wakened the old men. When they saw her making off with the cauldron, they called out two of the " coin-sìth " (fairy dogs).

The farmer's wife hurried on, but soon she heard the savage snarls of the dogs at her heels. She looked back in fear at the two animals—one green and one black—and putting her hand in the cauldron, threw them some of the scraps of food. This diverted their attention for a time, and she took to her heels again. Once more the dogs made up on her, and once more she threw them some of the food that was in the cauldron. As she neared the farm, the dogs were almost on her for the third time; so turning the cauldron upside down she left them with all that was in it, and made for home at utmost speed.

The farm dogs began to bark when they saw the " coin-sìth " which took fright and made off with their tails between their legs.

The fairy-woman came no more for the cauldron, neither did the fairies ever again bring trouble on the good wife.

The fairies of Seely Howe

A legend of Deeside tells how when the Laird of Blelack was preparing to leave home for the Jacobite Wars, he instructed a certain John Farquharson to rid his lands of a band of fairies who had their home in a hillock known as the " Seely Howe."

Farquharson had a reputation as a warlock, and was noted for his powers of dislodging fairies; but on this occasion, he found it more than usually difficult. This " Sìth " refused to leave the Seely Howe until he had provided them with another home. At last by his magic arts he succeeded in transporting them to the Hill o' Fare near Banchory.

The fairies, however, were unhappy in their new home, and unable by their own powers to return to the Seely Howe, pronounced two curses—one on Farquharson and one on the laird who had ordered their " flitting."

These have been preserved in local tradition in the following forms:—

" While corn and gorse grow to the air,
    John Farquharson and his seed shall thrive nae mair."
                    and

" Dule, dule to Blelack,
　　And dule to Blelack's heir,
　For driving us from the Seely Howe
　　To the cauld Hill o' Fare."

It is said that ill-luck has ever since dogged the steps of both Farquharson and the Laird of Blelack.

The dancer of Etive

More than two generations ago, two farmers of Druime-chothais in Glen Etive went one Hogmanay to Kingshouse to fetch whisky. When they were between Dalness and Ionmhareu-thuilain on the way home, they passed a *Sithean beag, cruinn, dubh* (a little round, blunt fairy hill). Night had fallen by this time, and through an open door on the hill, they saw a light and heard sweet music issuing from it, and the sound of a great company dancing. One of the farmers said:—" Let us enter and see what is going on here," but the other refused.

The first man entered the hill with his cask of whisky on his back, and the door closed behind him.

When an hour had passed and there was no sign of him, his friend became afraid, and went home and related what had happened. No one would believe him and he was accused of having murdered his companion. He was tried at court, but adhered always to the same story.

Eventually he was sent to Inveraray prison, and tried before the judges there; but they could make nothing of him, for still " Bhadaonnan an t—aon rud aige " (he always kept to the same statement).

Unable to find out any more than they knew when they arrested him, they let him go home. It was then October of the same year in which his companion had disappeared.

On Hallowe'en night, a number of men of the district were engaged in the dubious practice of " burning the rivers " between Ben Etive and Linge na Leuthchriege. To assist them in their night-work, they took a torch of withered pine and a great three-pronged " morghath " (fishing fork) carried by the man who had lost his friend.

Glancing in the direction of the hill, he saw a light issuing from it as before, and calling out to the others—"If you will not believe me, believe your own eyes; let us go and see what it is."

They made their way to the " Sithean," where they saw a great door standing wide open, and the sound of music and dancing within. The man with the fishing fork leapt forward and thrust it into the lintel above the door. The cold iron acted as a powerful " sìan " (charm). He entered the hill unmolested, and finding his companion still dancing with the cask of whisky on his back, seized him by the neck and dragged him to the door.

" Let me stay till I dance this reel," he pleaded. " It is not a minute since I came in." He was quite unaware that the reel had lasted from Hogmanay to Hallowe'en!

The man was taken home and returned to his family.

A Harris woman's baking

Told by Mr. George Ross, Corriemulzie, Sutherland

A Harris woman was walking along the sea-shore when, on passing a rock, she noticed an opening in its side, leading into a spacious cavern. A *beanshith* (fairy woman) was standing by the opening dressed in green and invited the woman to accompany her and visit a sick person inside the cave.

Although the woman thought the invitation a strange one, she duly accepted and entered, and found herself surrounded by a large company of " little people " for whom she was ordered to begin baking. She was handed only a small quantity of meal, but was confidently assured that when this was exhausted she would be allowed to go in peace. But the more she baked, the more meal there seemed to be in the barrel. Day after day she toiled to finish her baking, but each evening found her no nearer the end of her task than when she had begun.

One day the entire fairy company left the cave. It was the first time the woman had been left alone, and she paused from her irksome task to examine her prison more closely.

As she moved towards the innermost recess, she heard a moaning cry, which came from an incredibly old man lying

on a bed of straw on the stone floor. " What brings you here? "
he asked. She told him how she had been lured into the cavern
to attend to a sick person, and had instead been set to work on
the task of baking which seemed never ending.

" Begin once again," counselled the old man, " but this time
stop putting the dusting-meal back amongst your baking."

She carried out his instructions, and in no time the meal
was used up and she was able to quit the cave before the inhabitants returned.

The fairy flag

Every country has had its superstitions; and these superstitions have often been interwoven with that country's naval
and military glory. This is amply portrayed by the Fairy Flag
of the ancient Scandinavians. The Danes had a magical standard
called *Roe fans*, or " Am Fitheach " (The Raven.) It was said
to have been embroidered simultaneously by the three daughters
of Lodbroke (Loda), and sisters of Hinguar, or Ivar. But within
the Castle of Dunvegan in Skye has long been preserved one
of these enchanted flags. It came there through the Norwegian
ancestry of the Dunvegan family; and some very strange
superstitions have been attached to it.

One of these superstitions was, that wherever it was carried
into battle, the party which bore it would be victorious—but
this end being attained, an invisible being was to carry away
both standard and standard-bearer, never no more to be seen!
The family of Clan-y-Faitter possessed this dangerous office of
standard-bearer, and actually held their lands in Braccadale by
this singular tenure.

This Fairy Flag of the Macleods has been several times
produced. At one time when the family of Dunvegan maintained
an unequal combat against Clanranald, the enchanted colours
were produced and, it seems, the Macleods were multiplied
tenfold in the eyes of the Clanranalds! The consequence was
a victory on the side of Dunvegan. It was brought forward
again on a less war-like occasion. The Lady Macleod was

pregnant; she longed very much to view the Bratach Shith, or Fairy Standard. The charmed flag was produced to save the young heir of Dunvegan.

Cruggleton Castle has long been in ruins; but Dunvegan still stands. It still frowns with its ancient square tower over Loch Fallart, while another part of it displays the facade of a modernised Highland residence.

The bad fairy of Strathardle

Near the village of Kirkmichael, in Perthshire, there used to stand a large cairn called " Carn-na-Baoibh." It was said to be the grave of a bad fairy who did much mischief in the Strath. At last a great disease fell on the cattle, and many died. This was attributed to the wicked wishes of the " Baobh," and the people of Strathardle decided that she must die, but did not know how to catch her. One of the favourite amusements of the fairy was to make herself invisible, and to attend all social gatherings, funerals and church services. There she would slyly slap the cheek of one of those present, stick a needle into another, pinch another—until each was blaming his neighbour for the assault, and every gathering ended in turmoil.

This sort of thing went on for a long time till an old tailor discovered by accident the cause of the trouble. One Sunday, having to wait for the clergyman, the tailor took his shears from his pocket, he saw to his great astonishment the " Baobh " carrying on her usual tricks. After the service, he told the priest what he had seen. The good man adjured him to be silent; but to come to church next Sunday and bring his shears with him. The tailor promised to do so, but could not resist telling the story to his wife. She in turn told all her friends, and soon the " Baobh " herself heard that she had been found out, and that week, nearly all the cattle in the countryside sickened and died.

Next Sunday the priest carried with him to the service a bottle of holy water, and the tailor's shears. After a short time he looked through the finger-holes of the shears, and saw the

" Baobh " present. He called on the people to follow him, and set off in pursuit of her as she ran to the hill. Soon she sat down on a stone, thinking herself to be invisible. But the priest with the aid of the shears saw her, and poured the holy water round the stone in a circle from which she could not get out. She cried for mercy, promising to turn all the stones into gold, if he would set her free, but as the cairn grew higher he only answered by calling to his flock—" Cuiribh oirre, ouiribh cirre, clach air son gach mairt " (" Put on her, put on her a stone for every cow she killed ! ").

At the end of the last century, the laird of the surrounding district was in want of stones for drains which he had cut. Carn-na-Baoibh was ready to hand, and stone by stone it was demolished. No remains of the fairy were found; and contrary to local expectation, her race appears to have taken no revenge.

An gobha mor

The Big Smith

Many legends are associated with the name of *An Gobha Mor*, the Big Smith (or Armourer) of Polmaily in Glenurquhart.

He and his seven sons were noted for their great strength and for their skill in fashioning armour. Their " cold-iron swords " had no equal in Scotland. These coveted weapons were made from iron which had been heated and shaped by heavy and rapid blows from the hammer without the agency of fire. The Smith was also proud of his beautiful herd of cattle which were known far and wide. As if stricken by a fell disease, these suddenly and in a single night lost their good appearance and became lean and famished-looking, nor could the Smith find any means to better their condition.

Near Polmaily, at *Tor-na-sidhe*, was a favourite haunt of the fairies of Urquhart. One of these was the Smith's *leannan sith* (fairy mistress), and as they walked together in the woods one day, she told him how her fairy friends had stolen his beautiful cows, and had replaced them by fairy cattle. Enraged, the Smith armed himself with an axe, and rushed into the byre, determined to slay the unearthly herd. But before he could carry out his intention, the cattle escaped into the open. The Smith seized the tail of the hindmost and sped with them till they came to Carn-an-Rath in Ben-a-Gharbhlaich, near Achnababan. The side of the cairn opened to receive them, with the Smith at their heels.

The astonished man found himself in a vast room, glittering with jewels, and filled with articles of great value. The cows had now changed into fairies, and they asked him to choose what he pleased. He noticed in a corner a *loth pheallagach* (a little shaggy filly) which his fairy love had spoken of as having extraordinary powers, so he chose it.

The fairies gave him the *loth pheallagach*, but made him promise to use her only in the plough. For many years *An Gobha Mor* kept his word, and the filly was a marvel to the inhabitants of the Glen, for

> Threabhadh i Achadh-nam-bo,
> 'S an Lurga-mhor bho cheann gu ceann;
> Mar sin an Gortan-Ceapagach,
> Mu'n leagadh i as an crann!

> (Achnababan she could plough,
> And Lurgamore from east to west;
> Likewise Gorstan-keppagach,
> And still plough on without a rest!).

Alas, one day the Smith broke his promise to the fairies by yoking the filly to a cart, and she immediately lost all her wonderful power.

The gruagach of Arran

The glaistig was a mortal who had assumed a fairy nature. She liked to frequent human habitations, took part in domestic chores, and was always busiest at nightfall, keeping watch over cattle, or other farm animals, on the hillsides.

A glaistig who tended the cattle of the people of Arran was known as " a' ghruagach " (The Maiden). Offended by rough treatment she determined to leave the district. Placing her left foot on Beinn Bhuidhe in Arran she used Ailsa Craig as a stepping-stone from which to cross to the mainland! As she was moving her foot, a ship with three masts passed below her, and struck her on the thigh, causing her to lose her balance. She fell into the sea and was drowned, and "the people of Arran long mourned their friend."

This quaint story is told by the late Alexander Carmichael in his " Carmina-Gaedelica."

The glaistig at Sron-Charmaig

The glaistig attached to the house in Lorne was known as "Nic 'Ille Mbicheil" (i.e. a woman of the surname of Carmichael), and was said to have been a former mistress of the house. She lived in a ravine near the mansion, and when any misfortune was about to befall the family, set up a loud wailing. On sunny days she was often seen on a rock, keeping watch over the cattle in the fields.

One evening a woman dressed in green was encountered by the herdsman and his dog at a place called " Doire nan Each " (The Wood of the Horses), some miles from Sron-Charmaig. The dog gave chase, but the woman disappeared. The herdsman firmly believed that he had seen " Nic 'Ille Mhìcheil."

For more than a year before the old mansion was razed to the ground and a more modern building set up in its place, the glaistig seemed greatly disturbed. After the family had gone to bed she was heard walking up and down stairs and moving the furniture about. On the day the new house was completed, she set up an unusually loud wailing and then left. She has not been seen since.

The glaistig of Ardnadrochit

The following is one of Dr. Ratcliffe Barnett's stories, which he calls " The Good Glaistig."

A man of the name of Lamont lived at the farm of Ardna-drochit, near Loch Don in Mull. There was a glaistig at Ardnadrochit; and when a band of cattle-raiders came one day from Lorne on the mainland to " lift " Lamont's cattle, she changed herself into a sheep-dog and drove the herd up Glen Lirein. The cattle-thieves followed fast behind; so when she came to a place called " Glaic nan-Gaisgeach " (the Heroes' Hollow), the glaistig changed the cattle into grey stones (which are still pointed out to visitors on the island), and at the same time took upon herself the form of a stone. For a short time she and the cattle were safe from the raiders, but when the men reached " Glaic nan-Gaisgeach," one of them in his anger struck the stone that was the glaistig so hard that it split in two. That was the end of the Good Glaistig.

The urisk of Sgurr-a-Chaorainn

The urisk was a big, stupid, supernatural being, of solitary habits and harmless nature, which had its dwelling in remote localities. It was usually seen in the evening, sitting on a rock, " mor glas " (big and grey), and peering at the intruders. The urisk occasionally spoke to passers-by and it is even said to have attacked some; but as a rule it did not meddle with men.

A urisk once lived in a cave in a rock at the foot of Sgurr-a-Chaorainn in Lochaber. This urisk was a continual source of annoyance to the herdsman of Blar-a-Chaorainn. Not an evening did he pass but the urisk put its head out of a hole in the face of the rock, and hurled insults after him.

When this herdsman left Blar-a-Chaorainn, another called Donald Mór came in his place. He too was annoyed by the urisk which called from its dwelling in the rock, " Dhomhnuill Mhóir, cha toigh leam thu! " (Donald Mór, I do not like you).

One evening as he was returning cold and hungry from the hill, the cry came as usual:—" Dhomhnuill Mhóir, cha toigh leam thu! " Donald turned on his heel in wrath and bawled as loud as the urisk: " Cha'n 'eil sin ach comain duit! " (This is but the return you owe me). The urisk then ceased his jeering and from that day to this his voice has not been heard on Sgurr-a-Chaorainn.

Coire nan uruisgean

The urisks of Menteith—believed to have occupied " Cnoc nam Bocan " (Goblins' Knowe) on the south-eastern shore of the Lake of Menteith—are said to have been employed as drudges by a former Earl of Menteith, who set them the task of making the small peninsula known as Arnmauk, which juts out from the southern shore of the lake towards the island of Inchmahome.

In recognition of these services, and wishing to be on good terms with them, the Earl made them a grant of a steep hollow on the north shoulder of Ben Venue, surrounded by huge rocks and overhung with trees, which is to this day called " Coire nan Uruisgean " (Corrie of the Urisks).

At this wild romantic spot, we are told, the " solemn stated meetings " of all the urisks in Scotland were held—presumably until encroaching civilization drove them to seek still more seclusion.

Three urisks

A urisk used to haunt Beinn Dobhrain, a hill beloved by the Celtic Muse. It was said to live in summer time near the top, and in winter came down to the Straths near the village of Clifton at Tyndrum, where there is a waterfall known to this day as " Eas na h-Uruisg " (The Urisk's Cascade). This urisk is said to have been encountered by St. Fillan, who banished it to Rome.

In Glen Mallie in Lochaber, there is an eerie ravine called Eas Buidhe (The Yellow Waterfall); and a urisk—" Uruisg an Eas-Bhuidhe, 'Na shuidhe 'n Gleann Màiiidh " (The Urisk of Eas Buidhe, sitting in Glen Mallie)—was for long believed to haunt the spot, and proved very troublesome to the farm-servants in the summer pasture bothies near the ravine.

The urisk of Beinn Laoigh (Ben Loy), on the confines of Perthshire and Argyllshire, was often to be seen sitting on a stone called Clach na h-Uruisg' (The Urisk Stone) beside the Moraig waterfall, incessantly trying to prevent the waters from falling too fast over the rock!

The changeling of Yesnaby

" Trow tak' thee! " was till within recent years a common saying in the Northern Isles; it arose from the belief that the trows were formerly in the habit of stealing children and substituting sickly offspring of their own.

A farmer at Yesnaby had an infant son who fell sick and became very seriously ill. A local " wise woman " was called in, and after looking intently at the sick child, informed the parent that this was no child of theirs but a " croupin " or changeling brought by the trows. She gave them certain directions which they promised faithfully to carry out. At a certain hour on the following night, she said, the " croupin " would be in great distress, but they were to disregard its cries entirely, and were to keep something burning in the fire all night. Unless they did this, the spell would be broken.

About midnight, the child was heard to cry piteously, then seemed to be gasping for breath. It became blue in the face and the father, unable to look unmoved on its suffering, gave it a drink of water.

He appealed again to the old woman, who repeated her instructions as before. For the second time he promised to carry out her directions; but the next night the same thing happened, and unable to resist the agonising shrieks, he once more supplied the child with a drink of water.

The third night he resisted strenuously, as he had great faith in the old woman's powers. When no attention was paid to its cries, the " croupin " rolled out of its cot on to the floor, and with a piercing shriek disappeared up the chimney in a " blue-low " or flame. In its place lay the man's own child, sleeping peacefully.

This " blue-low " is referred to frequently by Ossian, and seems to have been a belief common to both Celtic and Norse folklore.

The trows of Papa Stour

In the centre of the island of Papa Stour, Shetland, are some curious-looking mounds, long famous as habitations of the trows. None but the boldest dared to venture near them after dark. One bleak night a man was passing the knowes on his way home when he heard a tune being played on a violin. Being a fiddler himself, he stopped to listen, that he might learn the " trowie-tune." As he was walking away whistling the melody, his ears were suddenly and sharply boxed by unseen hands, and through fright he immediately forgot the music and fled from the spot.

The trows of Papa Stour were also noted for their skill as dancers; and John Nicolson, in his " Folk-Tales and Legends of Shetland," tells of a woman on the island who every Yule night when the moon shone, used to stand on the " brig-stanes " in front of her house and watch the trows as they danced on the greensward near the shore. She sometimes invited her husband to witness this strange performance along with her, but, as Nicolson writes: " he never could behold the trowie dance until he either gripped his wife by the hand or placed his foot on hers."

An old tradition relates how the trows of Burrafirth built their " broch " or castle with stones taken from Papa Stour. They transported the large stones over the Sound by means of rafts; and according to the legend, one raft went ashore on the rocks at Burrafirth; and can still be seen at low tide sticking up in the sand with its load of stones.

The " blue " cows on Papa Stour are said to have been the trows' cattle and their rich milk-yield and sleek, fat condition are attributed to the fact that they were bewitched or charmed by their original owners.

This island seems to have suffered from a veritable " plague of trows," and as late as 1750 we have reports that there were so many of them living on the " scattald " (commons) that no one was safe to step outside the " toon dykes " after noon. At Yule-tide and at weddings they were said to turn out in such numbers that bands of them would stop the progress of the strongest men and sometimes kill them!

Kidnapped

Dr. Hibbert, in his " Description of the Shetland Isles " (1882), tells of a Shetlander, alive at the time, who had been carried to the hills by the trows.

He was transported to a lush meadow where a herd of cattle was grazing, and among them he recognised one of his own cows. He remembered the tales he had heard of trows found milking cattle in the byres, and taking to flight when discovered, leaving behind them curiously shaped copper cans; and realised at once the company he was in.

The story has rather an unsatisfactory ending, as Dr. Hibbert does not explain what the trows wanted with the man, nor how he managed to return from their realm.

But return he did—to be told by his neighbours that at the very time he had recognised his cow among the fairy herd, they had seen the animal fall over a rock into the sea!

The trows and the King's lady

There is an old Orcadian ballad that tells of a King in the east who fell in love with a lovely lady from the Western Isles, and after a short and tempestuous wooing brought her to his palace. Her name, we are told, was Isabel. The King was in the habit of going on long and hazardous expeditions in search of game. After one such foray, he returned to an empty palace. His lady had been carried off by the trows in his absence, and sad at heart, he set out in search of her.

" It is long, long he was seeking her. He had foam of the Eastern World and foam of the Western World under his prow. He saw the stars of the North and the stars of the South and the stars that are under the sea. He was searching through the blackness of night and the redness of dawn and all the colours of the day."

One day, in his wandering quest, he saw a company passing along a hillside, and recognised among them his lost bride. They proceeded to what looked like a gorgeous palace on the top of a hill, and the King followed them. When he reached the palace, it changed into a grey stone before his astonished gaze. He was an excellent musician, and the ballad tells us—

" Then he took out his pipes to play
But sore his heart with dole and wae."

He played like one inspired—first a sad song, then a glad song, and lastly " the good gabber reel."

The trows seem to have been as fond of music as their cousins the sith, for a messenger appeared from behind the grey stone and invited the King into the fairy hall. Once inside, he started to play once more, and was asked at the conclusion what reward he wished. He answered—

" What I will hae I will you tell
And that's my lady Isabel."

The trows could not refuse his request, and the King returned to his island home with his lady.

The last of the trows

When some of the older generations in Orkney wish any of their grandchildren to go on an errand after sundown, they may be heard to coax them with the remark that " All the trows are drowned now; they won't torment you any more." The explanation of the disappearance of the Orcadian fairies used to be prevalent throughout the Northern Isles.

The story goes that many, many years ago the trows became discontented with their homes on the mainland, and decided to take up their dwelling among the hills of Hoy. The " flitting " was to take place on a certain date at midnight, by the light of the full moon.

The trysting-place was the Black Craig of Stromness. Having reached it, they are said to have plaited a rope of straw long enough to stretch across the Sound. One end was made fast round the top of the Craig, and the other was seized by a long-legged trow known as the " Ferry-louper," who made an enormous jump which landed him on the opposite shore.

When the fairy company had reached the middle of the frail bridge, it collapsed, and the stormy sea overwhelmed them as they fell.

The " Ferry-louper " determined not to survive his friends, and taking a mighty leap into the angry waves, perished with them amid the foam.

No trows have been seen since.

2

HAUNTED HOUSES

Strange Highland happenings

U nder the heading " Folklore " are included all the antiquities, beliefs, customs, amusements, songs, stories, superstitions and common sayings of the people of any district or country. Concisely put, it may be defined as the study of tradition; but what I propose to deal with in this Chapter, is something different, something deeper, something shrouded in mystery.

In the Scottish Highlands strange things happen even today. In past years the Highland race held a firm belief in super-normal happenings; but such beliefs are tending to disappear, mainly due to the reconstruction of the roads, the development of industry, the hydro-electric schemes, and so forth, as well as the speeding up of everything, generally. " Och," said the gillie, " the electric light is frightening all the ghosts away."

The modern individual is apt to close his mind to the possibilities of anything unusual with a bearing on matters psychic; but there still exist unspoilt places in the more remote districts of the Highlands where old ideas and beliefs still linger and queer things do actually occur, and there is rarely smoke without fire. Every ghost story or fairy story is a factor in the history of the spiritual and ethical development of the human mind; but of course, one must naturally use one's intelligence in differentiating between mere legend and genuine miracle.

The ghosts of Ashintully

The Spalding lairds of Ashintully, Kirkmichael, Perthshire, were, many years ago, a wild and lawless family.

One of the Spaldings is said to have hanged a tinker on an old spruce tree in the castle grounds for trespassing on the estate. Before he died the tinker (a Robertson) put a curse on the family, prophesying that the house of Spalding would die out. This has been fulfilled. Some of the Spalding family were killed on the battlefield, while others died of mysterious maladies, and the estate has changed hands.

The hangman's tree still stands in the avenue leading up to the castle; and the ghost of the tinker still walks, shrieking his curse above the crying of the night wind.

The approach to the castle is haunted by another ghost—that of Crooked Davie. He was a hunch-back retainer of the Spaldings—famed for his speed of foot, and used by the Chief for conveying messages from place to place. He also met his death under peculiar circumstances.

It happened that the Spaldings of that time had a particularly important message which had to be conveyed to Edinburgh, and " Crooked Davie " was commissioned to carry it. On the evening of the day he was ordered to go to Edinburgh there was a banquet at the castle, and as he had a sweetheart among the maids, Crooked Davie was especially speedy in carrying out his orders. So fast did he go and come that he was back in Ashintully Castle that evening. The task had been a heavy one, and, being exhausted, he fell asleep in front of the fire in the great hall. Spalding came past and seeing papers—in reality the answer to his message—sticking out of his coat, thought that Crooked Davie had failed to obey his instructions, and slew him on the spot.

According to the legend, the shade of Crooked Davie still wanders among the spruce trees in the castle grounds, seeking vengeance on the house of Spalding.

Perhaps the best known of Ashintully Castle ghosts is that of " Green Jean." The story goes that the lands and castle were at one time occupied by a girl named Jean whose uncle, jealous of her position, made plans to have her murdered. One evening while her maid was combing her hair, her uncle entered the room and cut her throat. She was wearing green—the " unlucky colour "—at the time.

To prevent the murder being discovered he also killed the maid and disposed of her body by pushing it up the chimney, which has never since " drawn." He then dragged Jean down the stairs.

To this day, muffled but distinct footsteps are heard in the passages of the castle.

The small, walled-in private burial ground of Ashintully is also reputed to be haunted by the ghost of " Green Jean," who stands at the headstone erected to her earthly prototype in that weird, uncanny place amid dark pine trees and rank vegetation. My own dog refused to enter the spot.

Ashintully Castle is said to be one of the most ghost-ridden places in Scotland. There are a multitude of lesser-known shades which linger in its corridors and flit through the grounds in the mysterious underground passages between Ashintully and Whitefield Castle.

Appointment at Ticonderoga

Early in the eighteenth century, at a ford on a river near Balcardine Castle in Argyll, Stewart of Appin suddenly came face to face with his old enemy, Donald Campbell. Both men drew their dirks, and there was a bitter fight to the death. At last Stewart stood wiping his blade on the grass as the body of the Campbell floated gently away downstream. Knowing that within a matter of hours the Clan Campbell would be out for his blood, Stewart decided to rely upon the ancient law of Highland hospitality whereby any man (no matter what crime he had committed) could always count himself safe while being entertained under the roof of a Highland home.

With an ironic smile he set off—and a little while later was knocking on the door of Inverawe House, the home of Duncan Campbell of Inverawe, the brother of the man he had murdered. In all innocence Campbell invited him in and gave him the hospitality of his house. That night Campbell woke in the small hours to see with horror and alarm the pale, bloodstained figure of his brother standing at the foot of the bed.

" You are sheltering my murderer," said the spectre. " I insist upon revenge."

Campbell turned the matter over and over in his mind, but could not bring himself to violate the time-honoured code of hospitality. Upon three successive nights the ghost stood at his bedside, and before finally vanishing it raised its hand and with great emphasis and reproach uttered the words—" never before heard in Inverawe House, nor indeed in all Argyll "— " Meet me in Ticonderoga! "

The injunction meant nothing to Duncan Campbell. Soon after the safe departure from his house of Stewart of Appin, Campbell himself left to join the 42nd Highland Regiment (The Black Watch) with which he fought in France. Years later the Black Watch were sent to America, and there they were posted to a place lying between the states of New York and Vermont— a fort occupied by the French and called by the Indians " Ticonderoga." On 17th July, 1758, the Black Watch attacked, and Duncan Campbell of Inverawe kept his appointment made years before in Scotland by the sinister figure at the foot of his bed. The same night, in Inverawe House, a little boy awoke in a great fright to see a tall Highlander bending over the bed in which his father slept. In the morning he mentioned it to his father, who deduced that the visitor had been their kinsman Duncan Campbell come to tell them of his death in America.

It is said in the neighbourhood that the ghost of Inverawe House is not yet at rest. Local people say it can often be seen— a tall handsome figure in the Highland uniform of two centuries ago, silently pacing the interior of the now ruined house.

Duntroon Castle

On a promontory of Crinan Loch, a few miles south of Craignish, stands the old castle of Duntroon, commemorated in the pipe tune called " The sound of the waves against Duntroon Castle." In the seventeenth century Left-handed Coll invaded Argyll with his followers. He intended to attack Duntroon Castle and sent his piper on ahead to spy out the land. The piper was admitted to the castle and pleased the garrison by his playing. He took careful note of the lay-out of the castle, and then entered a turret to see how the land lay. But his presence there was discovered and he was shut into the tiny room with only his pipes for company. The days passed, and Left-handed Coll and his men became impatient. They set sail for Craignish.

From his turret window the piper saw the galleys in the Sound of Jura and fearing his leader might fall into a trap began to play on his chanter the tune known as " The piper's warning to his master." The sound of the music drifted across the water to the galley; Coll understood the message and turned away from the attack. But the man who had given him the warning was taken to the castle kitchen and there had his fingers cut off. He died from shock and loss of blood and was buried under the kitchen floor where a slab marking the grave can be seen to this day.

It is said that his ghost still haunts the turret room from whose narrow window can be heard the sounds of the fatal pipe tune.

The eavesdropper

This account of an Inverness-shire haunting is included
by the courtesy of the late Mr. J. W. Herries, J.P.,
Edinburgh

The following story of the haunting of a Highland House was told to me by a well-known Edinburgh business man. The house is situated on the shores of Loch Ness. It is a fine old residence, approached by an avenue of trees, and when built, some time before the battle of Culloden in 1746, it must have been a handsome and notable building.

A few years ago the narrator of the story spent a fortnight in the house. After being in residence for a day or so, he began to be aware that there was something unusual about the house. The people in the district gave him this impression. He sensed an attitude of expectancy or curiosity. At the local post office, for example, he had been asked in what was intended to be a casual way, if everything was all right and how he enjoyed staying in the big house. He left after a fortnight feeling distinctly, from a variety of causes, that there was something out of the ordinary about the place.

His friend, a grim, dour lawyer, stayed on. In a few days something occurred to justify the subtle impression created. The lawyer and other members of his household were awakened one night by the most blood-curdling screams. The sound, for which there was no explanation whatever, made a deep impression on all of them. There was something tragic and inexpressibly distressing in the cries, something which completely upset all who heard them. It was one of the most unnerving sounds that the lawyer had ever listened to. They were glad when their holiday came to an end. Apparently this was not an isolated instance, and it fully explained the furtive inquiries and attitude of the people in the village. The lawyer made investigations, and was told a story traditionally associated with the house.

The story was that in one of the large rooms of the house a number of Highland Chieftains were discussing their plans on the night before the battle of Culloden. Their talk, of course, was secret. In the course of their sederunt one of them was attracted by a slight sound behind the panelling. He went to investigate and found a young woman, understood to be the daughter of the house. She was dragged out and put to death.

It was only on hearing this story that the lawyer remembered an incident on the party's arrival at the house. One of the ladies, on entering one of the rooms, had a shivering feeling and became very upset, exclaiming—" I do not like this room." It was afterwards discovered that this was the room in which the tragedy took place.

The green lady of Newton

Newton Castle, Blairgowrie, stands high up on the west side of the town overlooking the Sidlaw Hills to the south. It was ransacked by Cromwell and by Montrose and occupied by Royalist troops in 1745. The castle is supposed to have been built in the early part of the fourteenth century. It is possessed of a ghost in the form of a lady dressed in green. According to one old ballad " The Ladye Jean " was enamoured of a young chieftain who had jilted her, and resolved to win him back. All to no purpose, she decked herself in silks and satins and silver-buckled shoes. In vain she braided her sloe-black hair into shining coils with a golden comb, and twined it with pearls that matched the dazzling fairness of her skin. The heart of her former lover remained unmoved and night after night she sat alone in the north tower—" wi' her heart in a lowe at the thocht of her luve "—singing plaintive songs from setting of the sun till dawn of day.

After months had passed in this way, she decided to consult a " wise woman " who lived not far from the castle gates. The witch told her that the finest crimson silk and the costliest jewels were of no avail, and that, to win her lover back, she must be dressed in the fairies' cloth—" . . . the witchin' claith o' green." When the lady asked how this was to be accomplished, she was given explicit instructions. She was to cut a swathe of grass from the churchyard and a branch from the rowan-tree on the gallows-hill, and take her offering, tied with a plaited reed,

Tae the Coble Pule, 'tween the licht and the dark,
An' sit on the Corbie Stane.

She did as she had been told, and made her way alone at the twilight hour to the Corbie Stone, where she sat with closed eyes. At first she heard only the sighing of the wind through the tree branches; then an owl hooted over the eerie sighing, " and a roaring like a river in flood, which she knew for the whinnying of the water-kelpie in the Ericht."

Then laughter sounded in her ear. A chill wind eddied round her and a hundred icy fingers seemed to be pulling at her fine robes. She sat with closed eyes and as cold as death while the fairy weavers worked. At last the crowing of a cock heralded the dawn of another day, and when " the Ladye Jean " opened her eyes—

She was dinket oot frae head tae heel
In the witchin' claith o' green.

It had the blue of the sky in it, and the green of the sea, and the grey of the storm clouds; and it fell about her slender form in soft folds. On her feet were sandals twisted from the green marsh-grass; and her lovely hair, flowing like a dark river over her white shoulders, was bound with a fillet of green. Never had a more beautiful maiden been seen in all the King's realm. A light—" . . . that never was, on sea or land "—shone from her eyes and she moved like one in a dream.

Within Newton Castle, Lord Ronald waited for his bride. Soon she stood by him, still clad in her strange green gown.

The marriage ceremony proceeded and there was mirth and music in the wide halls of Newton. But, as Lord Ronald looked down at his bride, he saw that her gaze was distraught, and he felt her hand, in his, grow icy cold. She gave an unearthly cry, and swooned in his arms, exclaiming—

Wae's me for you, my ain true love,
That ever this should be;
But a mortal cauld is at my heart,
I fear that I maun dee.
An' I hear a soun' that I heard afore
When a' my leafu' lane,
Through the mirk midnicht tae' the morning licht
I sat on the Corbie Stane.

Sadly they carried her to the turret room, where they laid her on her bridal bed. She was buried on Knockie Hill, and a stone set at her head. And every year, on All Hallows' Eve—

That stane, when it hears the soun'
O' the midnicht bell frae the Paroch Kirk,
Turns three times roun' an' roun',
An' the Ladye Jean comes ott frae the mools
An' doon tae the Newton Hall.

"The Red Hanging Judge"

Many years ago a supreme magistrate named Am Breve Ruadh of the Hebrides, earned the local title of " The Red Hanging Judge," on account of the ruthless and vindictive sentences which he frequently imposed. The penalties he passed were so cruel that he was ultimately compelled to flee from the Lewis to shelter in North West Scotland. There he lived in seclusion for some time with an old woman in a lonely croft on the hillside overlooking Inverkirkaig Bay; but his whereabouts were ultimately discovered by a Lewisman named Asgaig who tracked him to the banks of a remote loch in Ross-shire where he stabbed the Judge to death. On account of this incident, the loch inherited the name of Loch Sgian Asgaig (modern spelling Sionsgaig)—" The Loch of Askaig's Knife."

The murderer trailed the Judge's body some miles distant over rough country and dug a grave near a croft at Inverkirkaig (on the coast road between Lochinver and Ullapool) marked by a long flat slab of reddish stone to this day.

Some time after the murder, Asgaig's dead body was found in a loch to the north-west of Badygyle by the road to Achiltibuie. This loch was named Loch Osgaig after him by his friends, and still retains the name.

Less than half-a-century ago, a Canadian relative of the present tenant of the croft, while on holiday at Inverkirkaig, raised the slab of stone one autumn afternoon and found underneath a number of beautiful pebbles. He collected a few of them and placed them on his bedroom mantelpiece in an upper room of the cottage.

That very same night a violent thunderstorm occurred, waking all the inhabitants of the neighbourhood. One peal of thunder alone is said to have reverberated amid the hills for over an hour and to this day, the event is referred to locally as " The night of the Storm." The croft shook and vibrated, the beds swayed to and fro, and the windows and doors rattled.

Suddenly, at the height of the storm, the crofter's brother and his wife, as they sat up in bed, beheld a bluish-green light on the mantelshelf where the pebbles lay. In a frenzy of bewilderment and fear, the crofter's brother leapt out of bed and seizing hold of his trophies threw them seaward out of the window. No sooner had he done so than the storm subsided, and a great calm reigned.

In the morning a search was made for the pebbles, but not a single one could be found.

According to local tradition, the Judge resented the interference with his grave and his earthly belongings.

Can it be that they are once again beneath the slab marking the lonely grave of Inverkirkaig?

Skibo

Before Andrew Carnegie bought Skibo Castle in Easter Ross, it is said its corridors often echoed to unearthly screams and the apparition of a terrified woman would go flitting through the house. The story goes that earlier last century the castle was left in charge of a manservant who induced a local girl to visit him there. One night she did not return home and it was widely believed that she had been murdered although nothing was found to incriminate the man. Shortly after he left and went abroad the hauntings began and went on for many years until while repairs were being carried out the bones of a woman were found embedded in the wall. The remains were buried in the local churchyard and thereafter it is said the haunting ceased.

A room in Rothiemurchus

Some years ago, an old mansion-house near Rothiemurchus, Aviemore, Inverness-shire, was rented as a shooting-lodge by a family from Edinburgh. They were delighted with the house and its winding passages, crooked staircases and curiously-shaped rooms. One of the rooms, however, had not been used as a bedroom for years, as " no one seemed able to sleep in it." An old manservant stoutly maintained that there was no ghost, but that the room was " droch " (evil). The room, however, was furnished as a bedroom, and assigned to one of the guests—a business man who declared he could sleep anywhere. The room had three electric lamps, and except for its quaint shape, seemed not in the least unusual.

The guest liked his quarters and sat smoking for a while beside the fire before going to bed. Soon a strange feeling of uneasiness crept over him, and a lamp on the window-sill seemed to have a hypnotic effect on him. He switched it off; then the others seemed to menace him, so that he broke into a cold sweat of fear. He put out the bed and table lamps, then went quietly to the door and opened it. A noise from another part of the house made him jump in panic, and as he turned back into the room the stove was blown out by an icy draught of wind. Terror-stricken, the man groped about in vain for the lights, then tried to reach the open door. The darkness seemed " peopled with malignant spirits," and on the way out he struck his head against the door. When he came to himself, he was on a couch in another room, with his head bandaged. The noise of his fall had aroused his host, who was anxious to learn what had happened. The guest shamefacedly told of his unaccountable feeling of terror, but declared that he had seen nothing.

The old servant was pressed to tell if he knew of any sinister event attached to the room; he unwillingly related the following story:—

About two hundred years before, the house had belonged to a Highland laird whose only son was " as a chaill " (deranged) and had been confined in that room. One day he had escaped, and meeting a servant girl on the stairs, had attacked and strangled her, and afterwards had thrown himself downstairs to his death.

The mystery of Sandwood

There is no road, not even a footpath, between Cape Wrath lighthouse and the haunted Bay of Sandwood—nothing but intricate rocky hills, burns and lochans. The Bay is the most north-westerly beach on the mainland of Great Britain and is situated roughly seven miles due south of the lighthouse. The district has been called " The Land of Mermaids "; and it is a perfect setting for such supernatural beings. Hundreds of waves rush constantly shorewards, falling exhausted upon a beach of great sand-dunes that stretches for miles in all directions. There is nothing for the eye but mingling shades of grey; and nothing for the ear but the rush and roar of the waves. Sign of life is nowhere visible. Travellers have told of " singing sands "; those of Sandwood do not sing, but only whisper as they slide over the hulks of ships lying half buried along the beach. Over all is a sense of unbelievable solitude and wonderment. The gulls scream overhead—like the souls of drowned mariners lured to their doom by the maidens of the sea.

Late one summer afternoon, a crofter and his son from Oldshore Mor set out with a pony to gather firewood from the lonely beach of Sandwood. They were the only human beings on the sands. It was beginning to grow dark, when the pony became suddenly restless, and in a twinkling a bearded man dressed in the uniform of a sailor appeared from nowhere, close beside them, and in a loud voice commanded the crofter and his son to leave his property alone. Horror-struck, they dropped the pieces of wood on the sand and fled with all speed with their sheltie. So clearly did they see this man before he vanished, clad in sea-boots, sailor's cap, and dark weather-beaten clothing, that they could actually count the brass buttons on his tunic.

In the early afternoon of Thursday, 8th August, 1949, a similar apparition manifested to several members of a fishing party and to a gillie from Garbet Hotel, Kinlochbervie, as they rounded one of the sand-dunes. They all saw him clearly—the figure of a sailor. In fact, they put the gillie's stalking glass on him, turn about, as he traversed the crest of a large sandy knoll. They all noticed the brass buttons on his tunic glinting in the sunlight, and saw that he wore a sailor's cap. Thinking the man might be a poacher, the gillie went to question him. When the gillie returned to the party, his face was ashen-white, as he tried to explain, as best he could, that there was no one there at all, nor even did he find the faintest imprint of any foot-marks in the sand other than his own.

Some years ago, Alexander Gunn, a small land-holder on the Kinlochbervie estate (who died in December, 1944), went in search of a missing sheep on Sandwood Beach with George Mackay and William MacLeod from Balchrick. It was a fine night with a bright moon as they walked along the sea shore. When they were approaching the two large rocks which stand about mid-way, they noticed some driftwood coming in with the tide. Anxious to obtain some, George Mackay suggested to Sandy Gunn that he should scramble over the eastmost rock in order to try to secure a fine plank. Just as Sandy set off, they saw distinctly, the outline of a man standing on the sand between the rocks. At first they thought he was Donald Macdonald from Polin, who had climbed down from the westmost rock; but when they approached him and saw his hairy countenance and whiskers, they knew he was a complete stranger. Sandy jumped from the rock and rushed back to join his friends, and for a few minutes they all stood rooted to the spot with fear; for there was something unearthly about the huge, black-whiskered man who had so suddenly manifested; but as they watched him, he slowly walked behind a ledge of rock and disappeared.

Fourteen days afterwards, an Irish boat was wrecked off Sandwood Bay and the body of one of the crew came ashore between the same two rocks. He was unshaven, and not only Sandy Gunn, but his two companions as well, who saw the body, had no difficulty in recognising it as that of the same man they had seen between the rocks a fortnight earlier.

One afternoon in July, 1953, while picnicking on the side of one of the dunes to the south-east of Sandwood Bay, three visitors from Edinburgh were somewhat startled when they suddenly saw a large bearded sailor gazing down on them from the crest of a nearby hillock. They clearly saw the apparition for about three minutes. The spectre then took one or two steps backwards, and vanished just as suddenly as it had appeared. There were no footprints on the sand.

Sandwood Cottage, on a high ridge facing Cape Wrath lighthouse, has been untenanted for many years, and is now in a ruinous condition. It is perhaps the most remote and solitary habitation in the whole of Scotland. There is neither road nor path to it. It is haunted. According to Sandy Gunn: " I had been at the sheep all day, and decided to sleep in Sandwood Cottage overnight. I entered the cottage as dusk was falling and after making myself a cup of tea, I locked and bolted the front door and went upstairs to the room above the kitchen, took off my clothes, extinguished the candle and went to bed. Just as I was going to sleep, I heard steps—distinct foot-falls padding about below. I got out of bed and put my ear to my bedroom door and heard footsteps going from room to room downstairs. As the tramping continued, I dressed, and with my candle in my hand I opened my bedroom door and descended the stairs. I carefully searched every room in the house, but found nothing. I went back to bed and heard no more that night." Mr. Gunn was perfectly convinced that there was no living creature—human or animal—with him in the cottage that night.

An Edinburgh citizen of high integrity and not given to exaggeration who received a small piece of wood from the broken staircase of Sandwood Cottage, as a souvenir from the most remote cottage in Scotland, has had more than one alarming experience in her city flat, since the keepsake reached her through the post. She says that strange things have been happening in her house: crockery tumbling on to the floor, and during the hours of darkness she has heard knocks, and the sound of heavy footsteps. On one occasion she sensed a strong smell of alcohol and tobacco-smoke, and caught the dim outline of a bearded sailor, who shook the curtains violently before vanishing. This lady is not given to exaggeration, and has never visited Sandwood Cottage. Nor did she have any knowledge of its alleged hauntings at the time when she received the small bit of wood through her letter box. She tells me she still has the relic locked up in one of the drawers of a cabinet in her sitting room.

Duntulm Castle, Skye

Duntulm Castle, in Skye, was for centuries past the ancient seat of the Lords of the Isles.

On the death of one of the Macdonald Chiefs, more than four hundred years ago, a dispute arose among his followers as to who his successor should be. There were two claimants to the honour—the son of the late Chief, arrogant and cruel, and his cousin, a brave and gallant young man who had proved himself a good soldier and leader. Finding themselves in a minority, the cousin and his adherents retired to Uist, where the inhabitants were on their side, to organise a plan for obtaining possession of Duntulm.

There was deep and deadly enmity between the two cousins, for they were rivals in love as well as in war. They were both suitors to the fair Margaret, ward of the late Chief. Under his will, she was to remain at Duntulm until she was of age when two courses were open to her—to marry the young Lord of the Isles or to become a nun. Margaret disliked the idea of being immured in a convent; but at the same time the idea of marriage with the late Chief's son was distasteful to her, as she had already fallen in love with his cousin, who was in the habit of sailing from Uist to Skye under cover of darkness to snatch a few hours in her company in the shadow of the castle walls.

On one such visit, he told her of a plan he had evolved for making himself master of Skye. He proposed to cross the sea at night with all his men, land quietly, then build up with stones every means of exit from the castle, and dig under its foundations until it fell, burying his enemies beneath its crumbling walls. Margaret approved of his scheme, and the lovers separated, full of hope for a speedy reunion.

This hope, alas, was never to be realised. Unseen by them, the crouching figure of one of the castle retainers had heard every word that was spoken at their secret tryst.

The time appointed for the attack soon arrived—a stormy night when thick clouds obscured the light of the moon, and the sound of distant thunder re-echoed from the rocks. The men embarked with their leader, and battled manfully with the wind and the waves till at length they reached the rocky coast of Skye. They disembarked, and were advancing swiftly and noiselessly when they saw a dark line moving towards them— and the Macdonalds were upon them! The invaders rushed forward to meet their foes, and also to meet their fate. After a short, determined fight, the would-be Chief found himself a prisoner. He was marched under the frowning portals of Duntulm into the presence of his cousin, who received him with mock courtesy, and with pretended apologies for offering him such poor accommodation, led him to the top of the highest turret of the building, and locked him in a tiny room which held only a table on which was a piece of salt beef, a loaf of bread, and a large jug.

For a time the unhappy man gave way to despair; then he began to feel hungry. The beef was very salt, and he soon became thirsty and reached out for the jug. It was empty. He sat for a while stunned and motionless, then he heard voices outside the door of his prison and a strange noise that he could not at first comprehend. As it continued, he understood it too well: it was the sound of masons building up the door of the room, just as he had contemplated building up the door of the castle.

A few months later, the lovely Margaret died heartbroken at a nearby convent. Her lover's ghost was for many years believed to haunt the gloomy Castle of Duntulm, where the death-groans could be heard echoing along the passages. It is said that the castle was abandoned by the Macdonalds about 1715 because the haunting had become so bad.

Many years later, when the turret was again opened, a skeleton was found grasping part of a stone water-jug. The other part had been ground to powder between the teeth of the thirst-maddened prisoner of Duntulm.

The Killiecrankie ghost

In 1689, Graham of Claverhouse, lately created Lord Dundee, hung, with a band of Highlanders, on the mountains of Athole, in order to prevent General Mackay from taking possession of Blair Castle. On the night previous to the battle of Killiecrankie, Dundee had retired to his tent, to enjoy a few hours sleep. While he slept, a man with his head crimsoned with blood, started up before him, and bade him arise. Graham rose upon his elbow, but, seeing no human being in his tent, again addressed himself to sleep. Soon after, however, the same figure seemed to rise before him, and pointing to its own bloody head, sternly ordered Dundee to remember Brown of Priesthill. The commander, starting up to his feet, and laying his hand upon his sword, demanded of the guard, nigh to the door of his tent if any person had been seen to enter. On being assured of the contrary, he again composed himself to rest, not, however, without some palpitation. On falling asleep the third time, however, the same awful personage arose before him, and advancing close to his pillow, more sternly cried, " Arise ! " and pointing to the plain of Killiecrankie, which lay at some distance beneath, cried, with a stamp and a frown, " I'll meet thee yonder ! "

Dundee attempted to sleep no longer, but calling up a Highland chief related to him the strange visits he had received, ordering the chieftain, however, never to reveal the secret, if the coming battle should prove the Highlanders successful.

It is recorded by history that, on the forenoon of the day on which the battle of Killiecrankie was fought, Dundee never would descend from the mountains, although his men were somewhat galled by the fire of Mackay's troops, and a Highlander now and then falling at the feet of his fellows.

Whether he had any secret dread of disaster, or whether he wished no close encounter to commence until sunset, when his troops, if defeated, might find shelter in the mountains, will never be known. It was, however, nigh to sunset when he suffered or ordered his impatient Celts to fall upon the forces of Mackay. Like the burst of an Athole torrent, their onset was irresistible.

In a few moments the forces of King William were defeated, and beginning to fly, when a shot perforated the side of Claverhouse while lifting his arm to point the pursuit of the flying enemy. A little after, he fainted and fell, and in the very moment of victory, the cause of the abdicated Stuart was lost for ever.

The shade of Priesthill had also its revenge. Like the spectre which summoned Brutus to Philippi, the more awful eidolon of Brown had its triumph, even in the hour of victory, instead of the gloom of the offender's defeat. The hordes of the Highlanders fled, as if in exile, to their native mountain fastnesses.

Mackay, though defeated, enjoyed the substantial victory, and a little grey stone was erected to mark the spot where the victorious persecutor breathed his last.

The grey-haired grandsires of Athole yet recite to the southern traveller the awful dreams which disturbed the repose of the bloody Claverhouse, and the confidant, to whom these dreams were entrusted, held himself as no longer bound to secrecy, after the blood of his comrade had crimsoned the battlefield.

The lady in blue

A business man, with his secretary and dog, was stranded when his car broke down late one autumn night in a dreary West Highland glen, far from a railway station. He ran the car on to the grass by the side of the road. A short way ahead was a footpath leading down to the side of a loch, on the shore of which stood an ancient mansion-house, partly in ruins, which afforded the only available shelter for the night. After making their way past a disused churchyard they crossed a wind-swept moor, with here and there long grey slabs of rock and heather, which dipped down to the water's edge, and at last they reached the house.

The steps leading into what had been the hall appeared in the rays of their torches as if many feet had trodden them in the past, and the thick oak beams overhead were bleached by centuries of weather. These beams supported what appeared to have been the heavily timbered floor of a large room on the right of the staircase. There were the remains of two high fireplaces, one at either end of the hall. One was bricked up; the other looked utterly derelict. Above the hall ran a gallery which cast long deep shadows on the floor beneath.

After eating the food they had brought with them, they decided to get what sleep they could in the uncomfortable surroundings. The secretary remained in the great hall; and her employer, with his dog, retired to a corner of the gallery, facing the old bricked-up hearth. The dog was uneasy at first; but eventually snuggled down beside its master.

The dog's angry snarl, and the hoot of an owl suddenly awakened the man. It was midnight, and the darkness was so complete that he could almost feel it pressing on him. He became aware that someone was walking across the hall. He heard the creaking of loose floor-boards, and as the beams of the lately risen moon grew stronger, he made out a figure crouching by the bricked-up fireplace. He called out; and his shout was answered by a scream from his secretary below.

The dim figure resolved itself into that of a tall woman wearing a blue gown, who seemed to be clutching at the brick-work of the fireplace in a vain effort to dislodge it. She then disappeared as if into space, and once more growls sounded from the dog, and a voice from below called out again. Then a deadly stillness brooded over the ruin, and the air blew chill. The unearthly visitant had completely vanished, and the man was left staring at nothing. She had not passed him, and there

47

was no recess where she could have hidden. In the morning, his secretary said that she had seen a lady in a blue gown stealing silently along the gallery at dead of night, down the staircase, and over to the bricked-up hearth, where she had clutched feverishly at the bricks; but had vanished into space when she called out. On reaching the nearest village, they learned that they had spent the night in a reputedly haunted house, about which their informant told them the following story:—

The laird who owned the house long ago, was an exceedingly jealous man. His wife was very beautiful, and was much in love with someone else, whom she used to meet in secret.

Their secret meetings went on for some time; but returning home unexpectedly one evening after dark, the laird found his wife absent, and going in search of her, found her in her lover's arms somewhere in the grounds of the castle. He concealed himself in the shadows and took note of their actions. Unwonted bustle in the courtyard warned the lovers that the laird's men had returned, and the lady gave her companion whispered instructions where to hide.

The lady was wearing a blue gown, and later on, when she joined her husband in the great hall, he ironically complimented her on donning such a beautiful dress in honour of his return, and asked her to sup with him.

Meantime, his men ran all over the grounds with torches in hand to discover the whereabouts of her lover; but were unsuccessful.

It was a cold night, and the laird called for a second fire to be lit. The lady cried out that this was quite unnecessary, and a waste of fuel; but her apprehensive glances towards the second fireplace had told her husband all he needed to know about her lover's hiding-place. He at once agreed with her that two fires were unnecessary, and gave orders for the fireplace on the east side to be bricked up at once. It was sealed in front of her eyes, while her husband feasted in the best of humour.

At dead of night she came down to try to pull out the bricks to free her lover, who had concealed himself in the wide chimney; but by that time the mortar had hardened, and he was consigned to a lingering death from hunger and thirst in his bricked-up prison. She tried for several nights in succession to free him; but without avail, and finally she pined away and died.

According to local tradition, the unhappy shade of the Lady in Blue haunts the tomb of her lover to this day, clutching at the brickwork in a vain endeavour to free him.

The curse of Lochgarry

Donald Macdonald of Lochgarry was one of the most devoted followers of " Bonnie Prince Charlie," and after the terrible defeat of the Stuarts at Culloden he accompanied his master to France.

His wife, Isabella Gordon of Glenlivet, and his three sons, were not long allowed to remain in peace at Lochgarry. The Duke of Cumberland marched against the estate, and Isabella, disguised as a man in Highland Dress, managed to escape with her sons just as the marauders entered the castle, which they burned to the ground. The fugitives joined Lochgarry in Paris. Thereupon Macdonald vowed that never would he set foot on British soil till the Stuarts were again on the throne. He procured commissions for his two eldest sons—John and Alexander—in the Garde Ecossais, and Peter, the youngest, was placed in the Swiss Guard.

In course of time, his youngest son died, and when the Scots Guard was disbanded, Alexander entered the Portuguese army. John, however, being less sturdy a Jacobite than his father, determined to return to Britain. When Macdonald heard of his son's intended defection, he called down upon him the fearful malediction known as " The Curse of Lochgarry ":—

" My curse on any of my race who puts his foot again on British shore; my double curse on him who of my race may submit to the Guelph; and my deadliest curse on him who may try to regain Lochgarry."

Then, throwing his dirk after John's receding figure, he turned his back for ever on his eldest son, and shortly afterwards died.

Undaunted by his father's curse, John became a colonel in the British Army, obtained possession of his hereditary estates, and built a house on the site of the old castle.

As soon as he took possession of the house, however, strange things began to happen. The servants declared that at night the wraith of old Lochgarry flitted from room to room; bells rang from time to time; and there were ghostly knockings at the hall door.

The whole household was alarmed, the colonel's health gave way, and he eventually shut up the house, resigned his commission, and returned to France, where he died shortly afterwards.

The house remained closed till after the death of Alexander Macdonald, whose widow, a Portuguese lady, and her only son Anthony, came to take possession in 1812. Anthony entered the British Army, and brought his young wife to live at Lochgarry.

The dreadful curse of the old Laird seemed to follow them, however; for once again the disturbances began. The young people were forced to leave the haunted house; Anthony sold his inheritance; and also died at an early age.

The ghost of Noltland

Noltland Castle on Westray, Orkney, is a ruin dating from 1422. Its history is bound up with that of the Balfour family.

When it was in the possession of Sir Gilbert Balfour, Master of Queen Mary's household and Sheriff of Orkney, Mary seems to have intended to take refuge in it after her escape from her prison on Loch Leven. The walls never sheltered the Queen, but afforded sanctuary many years later to the remnants of the army of Montrose.

Noltland was believed to have a ghost—a friendly old man who took an interest in the affairs of the family and was often seen walking round the Castle precincts examining things in a leisurely way.

The extravagance of the Balfour lairds drove them to seek a humbler home, and Noltland was left to decay. Now the moss of years is on the walls, and the winds whistle mournfully through the empty rooms where the white owl has her nest.

The ghost of Noltland is no longer seen; but a haunting

of a different kind is associated with the ruins—a spectral illumination. It is believed to herald the births and marriages of the Balfours.

The Castle of Dunphail

At the time when Thomas Randolph, first Earl of Moray, owned the land on the left bank of the Findhorn from Downduff onwards, the whole right bank from Logie Bridge to the plain of Forres was in the possession of the Cummings. A feud arose between the Cummings and the Earl over the right to hunt in Darnaway Forest, and young Alasdair Cumming of Dunphail rashly determined to make war against Randolph. He set out with an army of about 1,000 men for Darnaway, without encountering any opposition; but Randolph had been informed of their plan by a traitor, and had laid an ambush for them in the deep ravine of the abandoned watercourse at Whitemyre. The Cummings were surprised in the dark recesses of the grassy gorge, and although they fought hard, they were soon overcome.

" It was a dismal sight that day at the river-side—the Cummings trying to carry their wounded across the water by swimming, and Randolph's men clubbing the head of every struggling swimmer who approached the opposite bank." Young Alistair threw his standard across the stream and with four of his followers, leapt the chasm and disappeared in the wilds of the Divie.

Randolph closely besieged the Castle of Dunphail; but one night, Alistair and his companions succeeded in dropping sacks of meal over the wall to the starving garrison. Randolph, however, tracked down the fugitives to their hiding place in a cave in the old bed of the Divie, over the mouth of which he heaped brushwood and set it on fire, refusing Alistair's request to be allowed to come out and die by the sword. They were smoked to death, and according to the legend their heads were cut off and flung over the garrison wall of the castle, with the cruel taunt—" Here is beef for your bannocks ! "

Weak and famished as they were, the gallant defenders tried to make a final sortie; but were cut to pieces by Randolph's men.

The castle ruins, since that day, are said to have often resounded to the clashing of steel and the groans of the dying, and the severed heads of Alistair and his companions are believed to appear at frequent intervals.

In confirmation of this tale, a green mound within the policies of Dunphail, on being opened some years ago, was found to be a grave containing five headless bodies.

Bonskeid

Many years ago, a native of Rannoch lived at Bonn-sgaed (Bonskeid) near Pitlochry. His wife was a Badenoch woman, who had brought servants with her from her own part of the country. Soon after the arrival of the new mistress and her staff, a series of unaccountable noises and experiences began to be heard and seen. Turnips and peats flew about the house, thrown by unseen hands; lights faded out; furniture was mysteriously moved out of position; bedclothes were unceremoniously pulled off; articles and personal belongings went missing.

In all these happenings, there was no appearance of human agency, and the whole affair was at once assumed to be the work of evil spirits.

When friends from Rannoch or Kirkmichael went to visit Bonskeid the hauntings were particularly bad.

On one such occasion, a spinning-wheel was seen to come downstairs step by step and dash itself to pieces on the floor.

The man of the house pieced it together again.

He endured these persecutions for more than a year, and was sadly broken in health and spirits by the trouble.

One day, before setting out on a day's shooting expedition, the tenant of the house, as he stood on the hearthstone before the fire, felt the stone begin to move under his feet. A " caileag dhubh " (dark hussy) from Badenoch was in the room at the time, watching him.

He saw her smiling; and it suddenly occurred to him that she might be at the bottom of all the bedevilment which had fallen on the house.

He lost no time in turning her out, with the rest of the Badenoch servants, and since that day there has been peace at Bonskeid.

Sandy

In Kinlochbervie is the tiny bothy where once dwelt the late Alexander Gunn, who shortly before his death was introduced to me by my friend Donald MacLeod, (now deceased) the former laird in the district, in June, 1939. Sandy, who boasted of never having had a bath in his life, was a most remarkable man, very intelligent, with an amazing gift of story-telling. He was the local shepherd, and had a vast store of legends, and was highly respected in the vicinity. He also had the " Second Sight."

Sandy died at midnight about 15 years ago inside his humble croft. That very instant, a cock crew, the roof of his dwelling appeared to be on fire, and was seen by many, a picture fell off his wall, and his alarm clock stopped at the very moment he breathed his last. The only thing that came out of that cottage was Sandy's own dead body. His cottage remains intact today, just as he left it, with all his earthly belongings still inside, just as they were up to the time of his death. His ghost is still said to haunt the building, and the local people will not enter it. I am told he was seen a few months ago, sitting on a chair by his bedside. But, knowing Sandy as I did, I am sure his ghost would be a friendly one.

The Big House

A story told by the late Miss Flora Macdonnell of Meoble, Morar.

Far away in the West Highlands there stands, surrounded by deep glens and precipitous mountains, a house at one time belonging to the Macdonalds of Clanranald, but now unoccupied. It is known locally as An Tigh Mor (The Big House).

Often on dark nights the whole of the west wing of the empty house is seen brilliantly lit; and those who investigate this phenomenon at close quarters have reported hearing doors in the house opening and shutting, although no human being appeared. At other times, the figure of a young lady in white, has been seen passing from the west to the east wing, and making her way to an attic. Many have guessed at her identity, which however to this day remains a mystery.

The grounds of this house are also haunted—a tall man dressed in a black cloak has been seen on several occasions. One night while on his way home, a keeper came in contact with this person, and having heard of the ghost, raised his gun to shoot. However, before he pulled the trigger, he remembered the old saying that a piece of silver placed on the muzzle of the gun would reveal what was really there. He reloaded the gun, this time, with a silver coin—and a horse appeared in place of the man! He fired at it, but without effect; the horse remained. Baffled, he lowered his gun, and as he did so the horse resumed the appearance of a man.

This ghostly figure is still said to haunt the grounds of The Big House.

The four-poster

Some years ago, an Edinburgh gentleman was on a fishing holiday in Perthshire. He took up his quarters at Tom Buidhe (Yellow Hillock), a mile or so south of Loch Glassie. One night when he had gone to bed early, he heard a sound in the room like someone sobbing.

The bed in which he lay was a huge four-poster with a canopy and curtains, which completely shut out all light. He listened intently. The sobbing grew louder, and the sound seemed to be approaching the bed. There was a swish of heavy drapery; the curtains at the foot of the bed were drawn aside by an unseen hand, and framed in the opening and silhouetted against a shaft of moonlight, he saw the face of a girl. He sat up in bed.

Standing before him was a tall young woman in a white dress. The moonlight shone on her neck and shoulders, and made a golden nimbus of her hair. Her eyes were big and dark and pleading, and she was wringing her hands in despair. Quietly the angler asked her what was wrong; but she answered not a word. For seconds only the man and the girl gazed at each other, then she sank to the floor, sobbing. The man got out of bed and lit the oil-lamp hanging from the ceiling; but by that time his ghostly visitor had disappeared. Not a trace of her could he find in the room, although for some time afterwards he could still hear the sound of sobs.

In the morning, he told his host and hostess of his strange experience. They expressed regret that he had been disturbed, and said that although several visitors had slept in that room, none had seen the ghost. They were able to explain her identity, however. Some years before, a servant-girl on a neighbouring farm had fallen in love with the son of the now " haunted " house. It was not certain that he returned her affection, for he was easily persuaded by his parents into marrying someone nearer his own social standing. On the day of the wedding, the rejected girl had drowned herself in the water-butt outside the house, and that night her wraith had appeared in the bridal chamber, sobbing and wringing her hands. The young farmer was unmoved by the apparition; but his bride of a few hours went mad, and died shortly afterwards.

Since that day, the ghost had not been seen, although on each anniversary of the occurrence, at the hour at which the suicide had taken place, the water in the butt had been heard to be disturbed. The name of the faithless lover had better not be disclosed, but it was thought that the ghost had reappeared to his namesake to seek from him the love and sympathy of which she had been deprived in life.

The green lady of Barrogil

There is a room in the tower of Barrogil Castle, Caithness, right at the top. Looking from the outside this room had a dummy window painted on the stonework, while inside you can see that the window has been walled up. Thereby hangs a tragic story. The bedroom is known as " Lady Fanny's room " owing to some confusion by the historians in linking Lady Fanny Sinclair, sister of the 19th Earl of Caithness and the last to live at Barrogil, with the daughter of a much earlier Earl, the fifth.

Four hundred years ago, this daughter of the Sinclair family, so the story goes, fell desperately in love with a young ploughman who worked the fields of Barrogil Farm, next door. Vowing that he would soon put a stop to the romance, the Earl locked his daughter in the top room of the tower. Discovering that she was spending her days gazing through the window at her lover as he worked in the fields, the Earl vowed he would stop that also, and bricked up the window, whereupon the unhappy girl threw herself from the remaining window to her death in the courtyard below.

No one knows if the story is true, or whether the Earl's daughter still appears in the castle as " The Green Lady." Barrogil is now the Scottish home of the Queen Mother, known as the Castle of Mey. Though the Queen Mother knows the story, she is not perturbed. Neither she nor any member of the staff has ever seen The Green Lady.

An Invergarry ghost

In Invergarry overlooking Loch Oich there is an isolated cottage, once the home of the chief of Clan Macdonnell. Prince Charles Edward is said to have used it as a resting place after the battle of Culloden. A few years ago it was inhabited by Mr. and Mrs. Andrew Ross. Mrs. Ross was then 77 and her son Duncan was 40. Both complained of hearing loud groaning noises during the night and one day Mrs. Ross suddenly saw the figure of a man in a dark old-fashioned suit and a lum hat, whom she at once recognised as the former owner of the house, Mr. Angus Maclean, who had died some thirty-seven years previously. " Mr. Maclean was a kindly man and I was not too afraid," said Mrs. Ross. " He peered towards me for a few seconds and then gradually disappeared. He has since appeared several times, always in the same place. Whenever I see him I get the impression he is looking for something." Mr. Ross, who is a retired gamekeeper, has never seen the ghost although the groans associated with it disturbed the mother and son a good deal, sounding " as if an old person were in great pain."

The swaying bed

This story was told by the late Mr. Donald Macleod of Kinlochbervie. Some years ago he was on holiday in Sutherland and asked for a room in the cottage opposite Gordonbush, Brora. As he was falling asleep he felt a chill wind blowing through the room and sensed the presence of something evil. After a few minutes he felt his bed slowly sinking down at the top left-hand corner and swaying as though the leg had been removed. He was petrified with fear and hid his head under the blankets. Before long he felt his pillow begin to wriggle beneath his head. Mustering all his courage he seized his Bible from the bedside table and sprang into the middle of the room. The door which he had locked closed with a loud bang. He recited the Lord's Prayer and gradually everything became quiet. Several other visitors have had similar experiences in this room, although as far as is known no tragedy is associated with it.

Hazelbrae

This is a story told by Mrs. Peggy Macleod, Sheigra, Kinlochbervie. In the house called Hazelbrae at Garve there lived a servant girl of whom her master was very fond. This made her mistress very jealous and one day she took some of her own linen and placed it in the servant girl's trunk. She then accused the girl of stealing and when the girl denied it took her husband up to the maid's bedroom and opened the trunk to reveal the missing linen. The servant girl threw her shawl over her head and ran from the house. She flung herself into the river from the top of the General Wade's bridge. Her body floated down to a pool at the back of " Hazelbrae " where it was recovered. Since then the bells have rung periodically in that house, operated by no human agency. The usual time is the same hour at which the girl took her life.

The haunted manse at Durness

As told to me by Mr. John Falconer, Achlyness, Sutherland, and corroborated by the late Mr. Donald MacLeod, The Old Manse, Kinlochbervie, Sutherland

Many years ago there were strange knocks each night on the manse door at Durness, then occupied by the Rev. D. Finletter, who on account of the phenomena was much perplexed and troubled in spirit.

He believed it was something unnatural, and being at a loss to know what to do, sent for the Rev. Thomas Fraser Ross, Kinlochbervie—the first Free Church minister of the Parish after the Disruption. The Rev. Ross rode on horseback all the way to Durness on Christmas Eve, and, not knowing why he had been sent for, tethered his horse in the stable and going into the manse, entered into friendly conversation with his colleague in the study. But the Rev. Donald Finletter concealed from the other minister the real reason for his sending for him. About midnight, the knocks came to the front door of the manse as usual, and making some excuse, the Durness minister asked his friend from Kinlochbervie to go to the door to see who was there. The Kinlochbervie minister unsuspectingly opened the door, not knowing who or what was about to meet him, and to his utter astonishment encountered on the threshold the ghastly figure of a man swathed in a shroud.

What passed during the interview between the minister and the ghost was never revealed; but after his talk on the threshold of the Durness Manse, the Rev. Thomas Fraser Ross went back to the sitting room with his face deathly white, and rebuked his colleague for not giving him proper warning of the haunting, for then he might have come to the manse prepared for the ordeal. So angry was the Kinlochbervie minister that he saddled his horse forthwith and set off for home in the dead of night. Shortly afterwards he became seriously ill, and died in his 46th year. His wife passed away not long after him. No rational explanation has been suggested for the haunting—or for the mysterious deaths that followed it.

A haunted house near Sleat

(This story was told to me by Kenneth Mackenzie, Clachtoll, Stoer, Sutherland)

Four men from Stoer, near Lochinver, went to work in Skye, and as they were unable to find lodgings for a few nights in a very remote spot at the back of Sleat, had to take up their quarters in a large house which had not been occupied for a long time.

After they had gone to bed, they were all awakened by a noise like barrels rolling down the stairs. " The house," interpolated the Gaelic-speaking narrator at this point, " was a very good house and had a good stair."

At first the men thought that some boys were playing tricks on them, but in the morning they asked a local man, who told them that the house was haunted by the spirit of a drover who had been killed in it many years before.

The men lost no time in seeking for other quarters.

Some time afterwards a ploughman and his aunt went to stay in the house; but they too were troubled by the same noises, and soon left.

The curse of Kylesku

Many years ago, after a wreck, a keg of whisky was washed ashore at Kerrachar Bay in Loch Cairnbawn. The cask was discovered by a local fisherman nicknamed " Tordeas, "who carried it into the old Ferryhouse at Kylesku (now the Kylesku Hotel).

After depositing the cask in an upstairs room on the west side of the Inn (access to which is gained by a wooden loft ladder) he invited some of his friends to come and share the contents with him.

During the orgy which followed, a " Seer " who was present prophesied a great calamity; but he was ridiculed by the other men, who simply laughed at such an idea. A drunken argument followed, and so heated did it become that " Tordeas " protested that the hour was drawing near to the Lord's Day.

His son, losing his temper, came to grips with his father and flung him headlong down the stairs. The fall broke his neck, and he died screaming out in agony: " My son, I shall return to have my revenge."

The son was found drowned in the shores of Loch Glencoul a few weeks later. Tordeas's revenge holds good to this day, for each year at midnight, on the anniversary of the occurrence, his ghost is said to appear at the entrance to the hotel " snuggery,' below the loft ladder leading up to the upstairs room.

Note.—Last person to see the ghost was the late Professor C. M. Joad, while staying at the Kylesku Ferry Inn about ten years ago. It is believed that the curse of Kylesku still manifests on occasions, even unto the present time.

Belfield House, Perth

A story told by Colonel J. Everard Rae, of Aberdeen

." In January, 1915, I was in command of the 2nd/1st Highland Artillery Brigade which was stationed in a school in Perth where the men were all billeted. The officers were billeted in a large house called ' Belfield ' about half-a-mile out of Perth.

' Belfield ' was a large, three-storied house. On the first floor, the officers dined; on the second floor they had their bedroom accommodation; and on the ground floor the men who were acting as officers' servants slept: there were about forty of them.

I was in Perth one night at the beginning of January—a bright frosty night with snow lying on the ground. I returned to ' Belfield ' about midnight, when I heard a considerable disturbance going on. I was very much annoyed, thinking it was some prank of the young subalterns. I thought, ' Will I go for them now or wait until morning? ' but decided to wait until the morning, and accordingly went to bed. Next morning I was down to breakfast at eight o'clock, which was the regular breakfast hour; but to my surprise found that hardly any preparations had been made for breakfast. I asked the Adjutant (Captain Ogilvie Shea) what was wrong and he said, ' Well, Sir, the men say that they have seen a ghost, and it has upset them very much.' I said, ' What on earth do you mean by a ghost? ' He replied, ' Well, Sir, I think you had better interview the head mess waiter, as he is the man who told me about it.'

The waiter came forward, and stated to me that in civil life he was a waiter in the Palace Hotel, Aberdeen, and had seen some very curious things in his experience there, and indicated that he was not a man easily upset by strange circumstances. He said that the men downstairs for some days back had been disturbed by knocking at the windows, and that the previous night they had arranged that they would all remain up, and that one-half of the men would remain at the windows to pull up the blinds when the knocking began, and the other half would be gathered round the doors ready to rush out and seize anyone whom they saw. At twelve o'clock, the usual knocking was heard at the windows. The mess waiter told me that the blinds were immediately pulled up, and that he, along with all the other men at the windows, saw a naked figure flit across the lawn and disappear into the woods. I asked him what he meant by ' flitting ' across the lawn; was the man running or walking across the lawn? He said, ' No, he was flitting.' I said, ' Did the men at the door catch him? ' He replied, ' No, they did not get him.' I said, ' Did he leave any footmarks on the snow? ' He said, ' No.'

Well, that is all my tale. Some of my young subalterns sat up one or two nights after this with revolvers, to see if they could see anything, but nothing more was heard of it, though I may say that a dozen officers' servants were so upset that they asked me to transfer them to the much harder work at the school, as they did not want to stay on longer at Belfield.

A week afterwards, I was in the Perth Club when a well-known Perth lawyer came up to me and said, ' I understand the Belfield ghost has appeared again? ' I said, ' What do you mean by the Belfield ghost? ' ' Well,' he said, ' don't you know how you happen to be occupying that house? Don't you know that we have not been able to let it for years on account of a knocking at the windows.' "

The Seer's warning

About fifty years ago, a man and his wife who had been staying at Kylesku Inn, decided late one winter night to set out for Inchnadamph. They were warned not to attempt the journey, but insisted on doing so. A local " Taibhsear " prophesied disaster if they went. On three successive days, he said, he had " seen " a drowning accident in Lochan Dubh. They scoffed at the idea, however, and set off in their dog-cart. Before they had travelled a hundred yards, a blinding snowstorm broke. Missing the road, they perished with the horse in the icy waters of the loch. If you do not wish to be frightened by what you may still see amongst the rushes by the roadside, it is a wise precaution to give Lochan Dubh a wide berth on dark nights.

My Lady Greensleeves

With Ruthven Castle, or Huntingtower in Perthshire, is associated the story of a " green " ghost known locally as " My Lady Greensleeves." This phantom seems to have been of kindly disposition, and several tales are on record of how she helped human beings who were in trouble.

In a lonely cottage on Huntingtower estate lived an old man with the reputation of being a miser, who was supposed to have great stores of wealth hidden away. One night as he was sitting alone by his peat fire, a band of masked robbers entered the cottage and demanded that he should hand over his gold or die a horrible death. In vain the old man protested that all the money he had in the house was a few shillings. They laid hold of him and dragged him out of doors, where they flung him to the ground and brandishing their dirks swore that they would kill him for having lied to them.

With a cry of despair, their victim stretched out his hands in supplication to a window in the castle. His assailants turned to look in the same direction, and saw framed in the opening the pale face of a woman with flashing eyes, clad in shimmering green silk. Throwing down their weapons, they rushed off into the darkness, and did not stop until they had reached the City of Perth.

Another story of this helpful ghost concerns a sick boy— the only son of a poor widow who lived in a cottage near the castle. A neighbour had gone to Perth for some medicine for the child; and the mother, fearing that he might be dead before it arrived, walked down the road to meet the neighbour returning. Seizing the medicine from his hand, she rushed with it back to the sick room, only to find the boy sitting up in bed, the fever quite away. His pain was gone; for a " bonnie leddy " wearing a green gown with pearl-encrusted sleeves had entered the room and stroked his head.

" My Lady Greensleeves " also acted as an augurer of the future, and especially of approaching death. One stormy winter night a traveller came to the door of Huntingtower seeking shelter from the blast. In the absence of the owner, he was conducted upstairs by the caretaker to a large bedroom in which a fire was blazing. He could not sleep for the noise of the storm outside. As the clock struck midnight, a tall lady dressed in green suddenly appeared in the room. She seemed to be in great grief, as she leant over the carved oak foot of the bed. Terror-stricken, the traveller gasped, " In God's name, who are you, lady? " For answer there was only a sob; and when the fire suddenly blazed up in the grate, the flame revealed that the green lady had vanished, leaving behind her only the traces of her tears on the counterpane. His shouts brought the caretaker hurrying to his room, and the two men spent the rest of the night by the kitchen fire.

Early next morning the traveller left for Perth, and when it became known a few days later that he had been drowned as he crossed the Tay, the country people were convinced that " My Lady Greensleeves " had come to warn him of his approaching death.

The vampire of Fealaar

The following strange story was told to me some years ago, by an old worthy of Straloch, Perthshire. An old bothy near Fealaar, between Atholl and the Braemar country, used to afford a welcome night's rest to weary travellers in the bleak and rugged district which surrounds it. When left unoccupied, it was often used by poachers.

About the year 1923, two poachers arrived at Fealaar one winter's night after a successful foray, and, finding the bothy door locked, broke a window in order to gain entrance. Once inside, they kindled a fire; but found that they had no water to cook a meal. One of them volunteered to go for some, and as the only exit was through the window, he put one leg over the sill. While in this position, he began to scream, and called to his companion that " some fiend " had got hold of his leg and was tearing it and sucking his blood.

After a violent struggle, he managed to extricate himself, and gained the ground, still in great terror and pain.

On searching the ground round the bothy, he could find no trace of any living thing; but saw in the distance white winged objects and faint blue lights which kept changing their position in the darkness.

With difficulty, he collected the water with all speed; but did not dare to return through the window, and, with the help of his friend, broke down the door. The two men spent the night in a state of fear.

Next morning, they could find no trace of man nor beast; their own footprints alone were visible.

The man bore the mark of this injury all his life, and it is believed that the unusual and unaccountable occurrence prevented any poachers taking up residence at Fealaar in after times.

It is said by some of the older inhabitants of the neighbourhood that the bothy has, to this date, the evil reputation of being haunted by " The Vampire of Fealaar."

The clutching hand

An Lamh Shanntach

A young lady, touring the Outer Hebrides, was making her way due south from Barvas (in Lewis) to Harris when she lost her way in the grey Atlantic mist and sought sanctuary in a remote cottage near Leverborough.

After supper with the crofter and his wife, she retired to her room. Something made her feel uneasy. The piteous howling of a dog mingled with the shriek of the night wind. She crossed to the window and closed it firmly, and bolted the door; but even then she did not feel safe. The candle was casting shadows on ceiling and floor; and she became aware of a curious musty odour in the room as of something long since dead. She lost no time in getting into bed, where, tired out, she soon fell asleep.

She was suddenly awakened by the loud moaning of the wind. There was a crash at the window, followed by the sound of broken glass falling on the floor. The window-blind billowed out into the room, and seemed to bring something with it—what, she did not know; but she realised that she was no longer alone. The smell of putrefaction was so strong she had difficulty in breathing. Once more the whines of a dog sounded from outside.

When she regained consciousness, she became aware of a cold, clammy hand that gripped her ankle with fingers of steel. Too terrified to move, she felt the hand travel to her throat. With a desperate courage born of the conviction that her last hour had come, she seized the hand, to find that it was attached to a sinewy arm that ended in space—there was no body at the end of it! Once more she fell back unconscious on her pillow.

Unconsciousness passed into healthy slumber, and she slept peacefully until morning. When she awoke she would have dismissed the episode of the clutching hand as a hideous dream, had not the broken window-pane remained as mute evidence that something other than the wind had entered her room the night before. When she recounted her horrible experience to her host at breakfast, he told her the following story:—

Many years before, an old bed-ridden woman lay dying in a four-poster bed in an upstairs room in the cottage, where she lived alone.

She had confided in her doctor that she had hidden all her worldly wealth—a bag full of gold coins—in the mattress of the bed on which she lay; and he, pretending to attend her, had slipped his hand under the bedclothes in order to secure the prize. As he did so, however, the dying woman started up from her coma. With her last breath she cursed the doctor in a flood of vituperative Gaelic—the gist of which was that his clutching arm should never find peace in the grave but should remain " earthbound " till the Day of Judgment!

The room in which the old woman had died became a " haunted room " once a year—on each anniversary of her death—when anyone who had the misfortune to sleep in it experienced the phenomenon of " The Clutching Hand."

In the excitement of welcoming an unexpected visitor, the crofter and his wife had quite forgotten the date, and had unwittingly sent their guest to sleep in the haunted room. They apologised profusely for their thoughtlessness.

According to local tradition, the doctor was the only one present at the old woman's death-bed. As she breathed her last, he drew the curtains round her. Her friends ordered the coffin to be sent to the house, and it was delivered by the local joiner (with whom the doctor was in league). When the mourners arrived on the day of the funeral, they found the box already closed down.

The bearers were heard to remark that the old woman must have wasted a lot in her last illness, as the coffin was so light; but it was duly interred with full religious rites. Only on returning to the cottage did they discover that the corpse was still in the curtained bed!

This necessitated another funeral—with another coffin—the following day; and this time her friends actually saw the old woman's remains placed in the box.

It was widely rumoured that the doctor, not daring to risk being seen leaving the cottage with the gold, had with the help of his accomplice smuggled it out in the first coffin, and later removed it from the grave.

Whatever may have been the truth of this story—believed to have emanated from the disgruntled joiner—the doctor disappeared the day after the funeral, and the gold with him. Neither was ever seen again.

The legend of An Cu Glas

The Phantom dog of Arisaig

Several centuries ago there were severe losses among the flocks in Morar and Arisaig. Shepherds kept vigil but failed to trace the marauders. One summer day, a crofter's wife left her baby outside her cottage in a cradle, while she went to the well to draw water—leaving her collie dog in charge. When the woman returned, she was horrified to find the cradle empty and the mutilated remains of her child strewn over her cottage pathway.

Believing the bitch to have been the culprit, her husband, on his return from work in the fields, dragged his dog into the woods, where he gouged out its eyes and beat it to death in a fit of rage and remorse, and afterwards returned and destroyed the litter of puppies.

Shortly afterwards, to his great regret, he discovered that his dog had been innocent. A black wolf was responsible for the crime.

Now, according to legend, a phantom hound is said to appear in the woods of Arisaig, seeking revenge upon mankind. Within comparatively recent times, visitors to the district have been confronted with the terrifying apparition of a huge shaggy dog with blazing blood-shot eyes, walking through the woods towards nightfall. This phantom is locally known as " An Cu Glas "—in Gaelic " the Grey Dog."

The ghost of Ardvreck

Some years ago, two crofters were going home to Elphin in the moonlight. One of them was J——— M———, a grand-uncle of a postmaster in the district. They were taking a cow home with them along the main road, and as they were approaching the ruined castle of Ardvreck they saw the tall, grey figure of a man coming out of the ruins. M———'s friend fled in terror, leaving him alone with the cow and the ghost! Feeling somewhat nervous, and not knowing what to do, M——— continued on his journey with the animal, which was becoming restive.

By the time he reached a part of the highway opposite the castle, the ghost was walking along the main road. The apparition was the first to speak, and remarked in Gaelic: " It's a fine night," to which M——— nervously replied that it was. The ghost and M——— then got into very friendly conversation and walked and chatted together for about a mile before the apparition disappeared into the darkness. M——— described the conversation as the most friendly one he had had for years, although he was reticent as to the subject of it. His phantom companion seems to have been a well-informed ghost, with a good knowledge of the Gaelic! The big, grey ghost of Ardvreck Castle has on occasions been seen since, among the ruins; but there are no further records of his conversing with passers-by.

Culloden House

Culloden House, which is passed on the way from the tiny railway station to the famous battlefield, is referred to locally as " The Castle." Inside Culloden House (at one time owned by Arthur Forbes, Esq.) were some fascinating relics of past days. The bed in which Prince Charlie slept prior to the battle, and his walking-stick, were carefully preserved, and there were also several swords, pistols, battle-axes, etc., which were picked up from time to time on the battlefield.

The present Culloden House was built in 1780, on the site of the old castle (part of it was destroyed by fire in 1947 and rebuilt in the Adam style). It is said to be haunted by the shade of Bonnie Prince Charlie.

Some years ago, the apparition was seen by the proprietrix, who had been in the habit of admitting the public to the house during the tourist season.

Returning from Inverness one evening, well after the hour for visitors, the lady was somewhat surprised, and a trifle annoyed, to see a tall figure clad in tartan with a plaid of hodden grey, walking along a corridor and entering the library at the far end. Knowing that he could not be making his way out of the building, as there was no exit beyond this, she hurried after the man in order to question him—only to find the room perfectly empty.

She immediately summoned her servants and enquired why a visitor had been admitted to the building after the appointed time.

The last of the tourists, she was informed, had left before six o'clock.

According to Miss Myra K. G. Warrand, 43 Bury Walk, Chelsea, S.W.3, a relative of the late proprietrix, her eldest sister, while residing at the castle, saw a figure of a man clad in " some dark kind of cloth," cross the second-floor landing. As the rooms on that floor were occupied only by women at that time, she felt rather alarmed, and was somewhat relieved when he suddenly vanished.

It is alleged that the same figure has been seen on occasions since, and it is believed to be the ghost of the Young Chevalier

The woman in the mirror

Strange and fearful things were said to be happening in and around an old house on the outskirts of Ardgay, Ross-shire.

A woman said that one night the kettle was lifted right off the peat fire by unseen hands in front of her eyes, and that she heard the pots and pans jumping about in the scullery.

So bad did these hauntings become, that she called upon the minister for protection. When he arrived in his dog-cart, a shower of loose stones descended as if from nowhere. This was followed by a battery of turnips and potatoes from the adjoining farmyard, but his reverence escaped being hit.

Bible in hand, the minister said in Gaelic:—" Whatever happens, I must exorcise this spirit," and being a courageous man, he volunteered to sleep in the haunted house.

When the door mysteriously burst open about midnight, he suddenly remembered he had left his Bible downstairs; so he went and brought it up and locked the door again.

Approaching the dressing-table, he saw reflected in the mirror the large black figure of a woman standing behind him in the room. When he turned round he was quite alone, although he could distinctly hear footsteps approaching nearer and nearer to where he stood in the candle-light.

He laid the Bible on the dressing-table and offered up a prayer, asking the unquiet spirit to go for good. Immediately it did so, and there was no more trouble.

Afterwards it was discovered that a maid-servant had suffocated her male child in a drawer in the dressing-chest, over eighty years before, in the very same room.

The bells of Kintessack

Near Kintessack in Morayshire is a house which has stood empty for many years, and is now crumbling to decay.

About the year 1850, so the story goes, the last of the old family of H——— died, and the house was advertised to let. It was beautifully situated in the valley of the Spey, and was soon rented by an Aberdeen merchant. Some old furniture and family portraits had been left in the house, and the newcomers removed these to a small room at the back of the dwelling, hanging the portraits round the walls.

One evening after they had settled in, they were disturbed by the violent ringing of a bell in this room. As no one was there at the time, no explanation could be found. The next night, at the same time, the bell rang again, and when one of the family went to investigate the matter, one of the portraits fell on him. The following night, bumping noises aroused the household and a trunk which had been standing in a passage was seen to be sliding downstairs, step by step.

Every day there were some strange happenings—keys disappeared, furniture was moved from one room to another, china was found in fragments, food was taken from the larder, fires were lit in the fireplaces, and in the beds at night were found thistles, whin, vegetables, and even garden implements.

Every day bells jangled and portraits fell, until the harrassed tenants could remain in the house no longer.

After they had decided to leave, the phenomena increased. They were afraid to venture into the back room, for each time the door was opened, a portrait fell with a bang, and the chairs began to move about the room.

On the day of their departure, not a bell rang, and when someone, greatly daring, opened the door of the sinister back room, not a portrait moved and the chairs remained decorously in their places.

This " haunting " has never been explained.

The evil house

A story from Polmaily, Glen Urquhart, Inverness-shire
told by the late Alexander Gunn, Shepherd, late of
Balchrick, Sutherland

When my services were accepted by Mr. Grant, the laird of Polmaily, he asked me where I would like to live. I pointed out a house opposite the farm and asked if there would be room for me there. The laird at once said " no," and on my enquiring why he said that it was haunted. I scoffed at this idea and a room was duly prepared for me. That first night I slept like a log. Next morning Mr. Grant said, " You are a brave man, Sandy," and gave me a dram. The second night I slept more peacefully than ever and again received a dram in the morning. On the third night about midnight I was suddenly awakened by a fearful noise as though all the windows and doors were being smashed in. The whole building vibrated as if in a violent storm. Overhead came a noise like a horse trampling and wallowing in the attic. I lit a candle by the bedside and I sensed strongly that some evil thing was present. I seized hold of my Bible for protection and drew the bedclothes up over my head. So far as I could judge the storm raged for five or six minutes. Everything loose in the house appeared to move and doors crashed open. I saw nothing. The next morning I told the gardener of my experience, who said he had spent a night in the place himself and that it was a " droch aìte " (an evil place).

I braved the situation in the house in the lonely glen for six weeks with the Bible each night under my pillow. The noises recurred on each successive third night. I can give no explanation of them, nor have I heard one since. The mystery remains a mystery still.

A house at Ardnadam

An Edinburgh lady on holiday in Argyllshire called on friends who had rented a house at Ardnadam (Ard-na-tuam—Height of the grave), north-west of Loch Loskin. As she was leaving after her visit, she asked her hostess who was the old man staying with her. The lady of the house replied that there was no one except her family. Her friend explained that as she was coming downstairs from the bedroom she had met an old man dressed in a white silk shirt and trousers, with a red sash round his waist and a red turban on his head. He stepped aside with a bow to let her pass, and she had seen that he was no foreigner but British, with a very wrinkled face.

Her story was thought to be very strange as she was an elderly, unimaginative woman.

Some months afterwards, the eldest son of the house came home from South America. Above the bedroom in which he slept there was an attic, used as a lumber-room. One morning at breakfast he said to his sisters, " What were you girls doing, dragging furniture round at one o'clock this morning? " They were astonished, for they had been in bed and asleep at that hour. Then their brother explained that he had heard someone overhead in the attic dragging furniture towards the door. Then he had heard the noise of the opening of a drawer, followed by what sounded like a revolver shot. No rational explanation could be found for any of the noises.

When the next quarter's rent fell due, the son called in person to pay it and told the owner of the house what had happened. The landlord expressed regret that they had been upset, and explained that an old army colonel had at one time occupied the house. He had lived for several years in India and on his retirement at Ardnadam, had dressed as their Edinburgh visitor had described. He had been eccentric. and early one morning his household had been awakened by a shot. He had piled boxes against the attic door, and when these were pushed aside, he was found lying dead with a revolver in his hand.

The Aultsigh inn

Exploration of the wooded slopes of the north-westerly shores of Loch Ness near Aultsigh (Half-Way House) brings to some tourists hours of exquisite bliss; but others who have had the misfortune of spending a night in the " haunted room " of the Inn, and have heard the legend connected therewith, have a different impression. The story of this haunting concerns two brothers—Alasdair and Malcolm Macdonnell—who both fell in love with a local girl, Annie Fraser. According to the story, both had made love to her.

One night, by pre-arrangement, Alasdair met Annie in a grove near the Aultsigh Burn—a picturesque stream on the boundary between Urquhart and Glenmoriston—a mile or two above the Inn. They climbed to a little circular lochan on the western shoulder of Mealfourvounie. But the younger brother had followed them; and their loving embrace was cruelly interrupted. Brandishing a dirk in his hand, Malcolm burst upon the lovers and challenged Alasdair to fight. A fearful struggle took place, while the girl who had encouraged them both stood white and shaking calling first to one and then to the other to desist. At last Malcolm overcame his opponent with a powerful thrust, and threw his body into the lochan. He then turned his attention to the girl. Disregarding her cries for mercy, he strangled her and trailed her body at dead of night down the track of the burn to the cottage which is now the Aultsigh Inn. He hid the remains under a plank of wood in the floor of a disused room. He then collected all his valuables (including a bag of gold) and made off to cross Loch Ness. That same night a severe storm rose, and a few yards from the shore his fragile craft was wrecked. He was drowned, and some months later the gold was washed up near Aultsigh.

There have been queer happenings in Aultsigh Inn, and visitors have testified to hearing in the stillness of the night footsteps as of someone moving slowly from side to side of the " haunted room " as if tirelessly searching for something. The " tannasg " (shade) of the unknown searcher has never been seen; but stories are current in the neighbourhood of the ghost of a girl with flashing eyes and raven hair—answering to the description of the faithless Annie Fraser—which haunts both the Inn and the surrounding district.

A house at Avoch

In the summer of 1937, a Glasgow business man rented, for the holiday season, a house near Avoch.

It had been standing empty for a year and when the house-factor showed the prospective tenant over it, he advised him against using a certain turret room as a bedroom, murmuring something about " noises." When the family settled in, the youngest son, a boy of 14 years of age, chose the turret room.

At breakfast some days later, the boy declared that someone had been in his room overnight. The position of his airgun had been altered, and he was sure that he had heard footsteps. He was told that he had been dreaming, and the incident was soon forgotten.

A week or so later, the lad said that some of his books had been tampered with, and that he had again heard footsteps in the dark. He was sure now that his brothers were playing a joke on him. He took his dog to his room and fastened him to the fender, thinking that he would be certain to bark when the " practical jokers " came into the room.

Some nights after, he was awakened by the now familiar footsteps, followed by a loud crash. He sat up in bed, and to his astonishment saw the faintly luminous figure of a youth of about his own age crossing from the door to the open turret window. The figure turned towards him, then disappeared as if he had fallen out of the window.

The dog, which had overturned the heavy iron fender in its fright, stood staring after the ghostly intruder, with every hair standing on end.

The boy called his father and brothers, and his tale (coupled with the evidence of the dog) was so convincing, that they searched the garden; but could find nothing to tell of any intruder. Later, they were told that three years before, while walking in his sleep, the only son of the owner of the house had been killed by a fall from the turret window, and that his ghost was still believed to " walk."

The wraith of Rait

Rait Castle, in Nairnshire, is by tradition the scene of grim tragedy. A long and deadly feud existed between the Cummings and the Mackintoshes. Both were powerful clans, and after many a bloody fight they were still unreconciled.

On one occasion, the Chief of the Cummings, pretending that he wished to forget former animosities and establish friendly relations, invited The Mackintosh and his followers to a grand banquet at Rait.

The invitation was accepted; but the Mackintoshes were warned in time that the Cummings had planned a foul plot by which, at a given signal, each Cumming would rise and slay one of the defenceless guests. They resolved, however, to attend the feast.

On the night of the banquet, " each Mackintosh hid his dirk in his plaid and gaily took his seat at the festive board of Cumming of Rait."

Suddenly, the door of the hall was thrown open, and preceded by a piper, a Cumming entered with a bullock's head on a charger. A toast was given—" To the memory of the dead." This was the signal agreed upon for the slaughter of the guests; but as the Cummings were about to draw their swords, the Mackintoshes sprang to their feet, drew their daggers, and plunged them into the hearts of their enemies.

Among the few who escaped death was the Chief of the Cummings. He made his way to an upper chamber where his daughter was, suspecting that it was she who had given warning to the Mackintoshes, as he knew that she and the young Mackintosh were secret lovers.

When she saw her father's rage, she tried to escape him, but he dragged her back and cut off her hands. Frantic with pain, she leapt to her death in the courtyard below.

From the night of the tragedy the blood-stained walls of Rait have been tenantless; but the villagers of Geddes speak to this day of sounds of clashing swords and groans of dying men heard coming from the ruin; and of the figure of a girl which wanders at night over the hill behind the castle, with blood trickling down her white dress—one of those nightmare visions—" that not only survive dawn but cloud the day." They call her the Wraith of Rait.

The phantom Druid of Kirkmichael

An English maid who was employed in the Old Manse, Kirkmichael, Perthshire, a good many years ago, twice had strange experiences there.

On the first occasion, in the early hours of the morning, she saw the figure of an old man standing by the window in her room, dressed in white flowing robes, crowned with a chaplet of leaves, and carrying a golden sickle.

Later, when alone in the house, she was terror-stricken by a sudden cry of anguish, which rose to a crescendo and then died shudderingly away.

No account was taken of these incidents at the time. The first was dismissed as the effect of the shifting shapes of morning mist on the mind of someone only half-awake; and the origin of the cry was traced to the presence of a barn owl, which had been trapped in one of the chimneys.

On further investigation, it was discovered that Kirkmichael Manse was said to stand on the site of " stones " set up by Druids as a place of worship—a worship in which human sacrifice was a main ingredient.

The coffin in Glen Fee

Towards the close of the eighteenth century, Charles Duncan, known as " The Stalker " on account of his ability and skill in deer-stalking, was gamekeeper to the Earl of Airlie.

On 21st September, 1817, he set out for Bachnagairn Forest, intending to meet a fellow-stalker, Peter MacKinnon, with the stag-hounds at the " Craw Craigies." He walked briskly along lower Glen Doll, whistling cheerfully as he went. He had almost reached the upper Glen when he noticed a large wild cat sitting among the heather. He quickly loaded his rifle and crept cautiously towards the cat. Unfortunately, he slipped on some loose stones and the animal made off.

The gamekeeper was just on the point of rushing after it when he happened to look round. In front of him was an expanse of long, rank, and deeply green grass, dotted here and there with the headstones of graves. Some were moss-grown and uncared for, while others looked new and fresh, with a few flowers beside them. He looked round in amazement, thinking he must be dreaming; and happening to glance down, saw near him an open coffin with a corpse in it. He felt completely bewildered. What was his horror to find that he was looking at an exact reproduction of his own face, although the features seemed those of an older man. Utter bewilderment rooted him to the spot, and he stared fascinated at the corpse. He turned round, but stumbled over something and fell on his face. He saw that he had kicked over the coffin-lid which had been resting against the side of the coffin. On the lid was a small brass plate, and he stooped to read the inscription. It read:—

IN MEMORY
OF
CHARLES DUNCAN
AGED 83 YEARS
21ST SEPT., 1848

Charles thought he must be out of his mind, and forced himself to leave the uncanny place. He set off steadily down the glen, threading his way among the heights and hollows at the side of Loch Fee; but kept looking fearfully back.

When he had recovered from the shock of his experience, Charles resumed his duties as stalker; but always avoided Loch Fee, nor would he approach Glen Doll alone.

Some years afterwards, a traveller on his way to one of the farms of Acharn, stopped for a few minutes at an inn, where he heard talk of a certain Charles Duncan—" The Stalker "—who had died that day at the age of eighty-three. It was the 21st of September, 1848.

The widow's curse

Some years ago, an Excise Officer was moved to a district in Easter Ross, and had to spend a night alone in his new quarters before being joined by his wife and family.

That night, shortly after midnight, he was wakened by a sound like the scampering of feet in an adjoining room. Attributing the noise to rats, he fell asleep again; but in a short time was wakened once more by the sound of someone noisily sweeping with a broom. For a time he lay and listened; then rose to light the lamp. Before he had struck a match, he heard a voice pleading in Gaelic, " Let me in, let me in."

No sooner, however, did he light the lamp than there was dead silence. Thinking that it had been a nightmare, he turned down the lamp again and fell asleep. This time he was awakened by a rattling door, and a feeble voice crying, " I cannot harm you; but leave this place soon, do, do."

Convinced this time of the reality of the voice, he dressed and left the house; wakened his nearest neighbour, and asked if he would come back and help him to examine the house. The man, however, refused to accompany him at that hour. As they waited for dawn to break, the neighbour (an old resident) told him that more than fifty years before, a poor widow had been forcibly evicted from her home to provide the site for the house; and had cursed the new building and all who would live in it. He told how, while it was in the course of erection, mysterious lights had been seen moving round it; how the workmen had found their tools scattered; how one tenant had become bankrupt; and how another had died in the house after two days' illness.

In the morning, the two men searched the house; but found no sign of disturbance, and no rational explanation of the mysterious happenings of the night before. The Excise Officer sought other quarters.

To this day, no native of the place will go near the house at night. It stands there gaunt and empty, a " naked house on a naked moor," waiting for a tenant who will brave the widow's curse.

Castle Grant

The " haunted room " at Castle Grant, Morayshire, is a small, normal looking bedroom in the old tower, reached by a stone stair, the steps of which are thickly carpeted with Ancient Grant tartan. The room is hung with tapestry, which is said to have been woven by twenty-two ladies who once lived there in exile.

At regular intervals, the figure of a lady is said to appear through the tapestry hangings on the wall. She is small and in no way terrifying. This shade goes through the action of washing her hands, and then darts across the room to disappear through a door leading to a winding staircase. Her identity has never been satisfactorily established, although one account identifies her as Barbara Grant, daughter of a sixteenth century laird. There is a dark closet opening off the tapestry room, and the story is that the girl was imprisoned there by her father for refusing to marry the bridegroom he had chosen for her. It is said that she died in her dark prison rather than yield her heart to a man whom she did not love.

A ghost who confessed

A story told by John Falconer, Achlyness, Sutherland

A young girl from Kinlochbervie, Sutherland, went as a servant to a house near Riconich for the summer months, leased by a father and two sons for the season's fishing.

The maid had not been long in service when, after a short illness, the old man died and was buried in a churchyard some miles distant. Then, in the words of the Gaelic-speaking narrator of the story—" There was something coming to the house every night afterwards."

So terrified were the occupants, that the two sons sent for the minister. He came, " but was greatly annoyed at the whole matter." At last he said: " Seeing that you asked me, I shall speak to him." He did so that night, and the apparition replied: " I gave a false oath at a crofter's house on a widow's bull " (i.e. he had pretended that the bull belonged to someone else) " and I can get no rest until I admit it."

The ghost, having thus confessed to the minister, never returned.

Dalarossie kirk

Adjoining the kirk at Dalarossie or Dalfergussie (Fergus's Valley) in the upper Findhorn valley there is a glebe on which there is an old story. A team of the Shaws of Strathnairn once challenged an equal number of Strathdurn men to a game of shinty. The match was fixed for Christmas Day which that year fell on a Sunday. The Shaws turned up at the appointed time but their opponents did not. Accordingly they picked sides from among themselves and proceeded with their game on the

Sabbath. It is said that within a year all the players in this unhallowed game were dead, and were buried in the level part of the churchyard next the river. When Christmas Day falls on a Sunday a phantom team is said to repeat the game on the glebe at dead of night.

Of the church itself there is a grim story about a skull which appears and disappears inside the building in a way no human being can explain.

An Islay ghost story

A man on holiday in the " Emerald Isle " of Islay, was a guest at a well-known distillery house not far from Port Ellen. On his way upstairs to bed with a candle in his hand, he saw a figure some paces ahead of him, walking in the same direction.

From the appearance of the figure, he knew that it could not be that of his host, who was a tall man. The person in front of him was short in stature and thick-set, and (so far as he could see by the light of the candle) was dressed in somewhat antiquated garb. For seconds the apparition remained, then melted into space at the far end of the passage. Its disappearance was followed by the noise of a dull, heavy thud; then there was silence.

Somewhat unnerved by what he had seen and heard, the guest made his way with all speed to his room.

That night he had a most vivid dream. He felt that something or someone was drawing him irresistibly towards a high window at the end of a passage. Struggle as he might, there was no escape. In his dream he caught at the furniture—the curtains —at anything he could lay hold of to stop this inexorable progress. Then he saw himself on a window-ledge, peering down into a sickening gulf. He felt himself falling and then woke up with a start to hear a clock striking five. He determined to say nothing to his host.

The next night, as he was going to bed, he was once more startled to see the shadowy figure preceding him along the corridor, only to disappear as before at the end of it. Again there was a heavy thud, followed by a silence so profound that it could almost be felt. Again he dreamed the same dream. He found himself moving step by step towards an open window. He could feel the night air on his brow. So vivid was this sensation that with a violent effort he awoke—to find himself at the end of the passage leading from his room, pressing with both hands against a blank wall.

He had never walked in his sleep before, and greatly perturbed, he told his host the whole story next morning. He was referred for an explanation to an old distillery worker, who told him how, over a hundred years ago, before the modern portion of the distillery building had been erected, a man had broken into the distillery at dead of night. Maddened by liquor, he had thrown himself out of an open window, and had been killed instantly. The window had since been walled up, and the modern part of the building added at the end of the corridor already referred to. The apparition was well known to be the earth-bound spirit of the man who had crashed to his death well over a hundred years before.

It is alleged that he haunts the distillery to this day.

Calum Breac

While on holiday in the north of Scotland a visitor arrived at the village of Achilty, Ross-shire, on an August evening after a long day's walk. He was directed to a lonely croft on an open stretch of moor, where he asked for a room for the night. He fell asleep immediately on going to bed but next morning appeared pale and tired. He said he had not slept very well. His host pressed him to tell what had happened and his guest then related how he had been awakened by footsteps, footsteps which sounded—and he quoted a Gaelic phrase: "Fuaim casan as a' mhointich "—" Like the sucking feet of the wet moss." Footsteps were followed by a terrible crash. "I saw nothing, but I sensed that there was something unearthly in my room," he went on. "There was a draught of cold air and a voice came out of the darkness, saying: ' I am Calum Breac,

follow me, that I may show you the reason for my visitation.'
At first I thought that it was yourself (his host) that was wanting
me. I got out of bed and went through the open door. I went
downstairs and when I found myself on the threshold of the
front door I felt an icy wind on my brow, although it was a
warm summer night. By this time I was fully awake and realised
that the voice I had heard had not been a human one. I rushed
back to my room and locked and bolted the door."

The host looked at his visitor and gave him a sympathetic
nod. " I am glad you did not see anything," he said. " I am
told the apparition takes a rather terrifying form. It is a tall
old man with angry eyes and a thick black beard. I have not
seen it myself and I have no idea why it should come here."

Two months later the cottage mysteriously took fire and
was completely burned out. Inside the bare walls it was noticed
that the lintel above the front door bore an inscription and
was, in fact, a headstone from the churchyard long disused.
The words read: " In memory of Calum Breac." This house
in Achilty was reconstructed about fifty years ago and, so far
as is known, still stands today.

Visitor from the sea

If on a Highland beach you should come across the belongings of a sailor washed ashore from a wreck, leave them lying
where they are. Should you pick them up the chances are that
the shade of the dead owner will come to ask you for them back.

One day at Sheigra in Kinlochbervie a crofter picked up the
belongings of a sailor drowned off the coast nearby. Some
nights later a strange man inexplicably appeared in his croft.
He was dressed as a sailor and after roaming about the room he
disappeared. The following night he came again and then on
several successive nights, each time staying a little longer than
before. In time he began to get obstreperous and started
upsetting the furniture.

The crofter became very alarmed and summoned the
minister, who advised that the ghost be asked what it was he

wanted. The crofter was afraid because of the belief that to converse with a spirit ensured death within a year. Finally he plucked up courage and spoke to the phantom who replied in Gaelic. Crofter and ghost then walked out of the croft together and went down to the sea-shore where the spirit walked into the water and slowly dissolved into mist. The crofter is still alive today. He will not tell what words passed between them but says only that the sailor went back to the sea satisfied and has not reappeared since.

The undead sailor

Three hundred years ago a Polish ship was driven ashore at Sandwood Bay in Sutherland. The survivors founded a village nearby called, to this day, " Polan " the place of the Poles. But not all the crew of the ship survived and it is said that the shade of one of them frequently knocks at the door of a certain cottage—one of them " who does not realise he is dead." Those who have unwisely opened the door and seen him standing on the threshold against the background of a storm-tossed sea have been horrified to see that he is headless.

The fisherman's hut

There is a disused fisherman's hut at a place known as Port Mor, West Sutherland, where the Loch à Mhuilinn Burn empties itself into the sea near Sandwood Bay. This hut is reputed to be haunted.

Some years ago a crew of fishermen beached in this bay. All but one walked home to their crofts at Droman and Polin, leaving the thirteenth man in charge of their gear.

As he was engaged in baking oatcakes that night, he was startled by the tramp of footsteps on the shingle outside, and shortly afterwards the tall dark figure of a sailor entered the hut and, after muttering in Gaelic, attacked him. The struggle lasted until dawn, when the ghost vanished, leaving the fisherman in a state of exhaustion.

Some time afterwards, it is said, another fisherman encountered the ghost while alone in the hut late one night; but when the fisherman made the Sign of the Cross and acknowledged himself to God, the spectre walked into the sea and disappeared.

This story is vouched for by Mr. Alexander MacLeod, Sheigra.

Strange tales of Stoer

Told by the Late Mrs. Mary MacLeod, Stoer, Sutherland. Mrs. MacLeod told all her stories in Gaelic, and I had great difficulty in taking notes. Even had she spoken in English, that would have been difficult as she spoke very quietly. She was very old at the time

A GHOST FUNERAL

" One dark night many years ago, I was coming home from Raffin with a friend. The hour was late, and we were walking at a good pace, when my friend's speed began to slacken, and for a time he refused to go more than at a snail's pace. Eventually, we came to where he had to branch off to his home, and he asked me to see him to his door. He did not say then what the matter was, as he didn't want to frighten me; but a day or two later, said that he had seen a ghost funeral, and sure enough, a funeral did pass along that road within the next few days."

AN INVERKIRKAIG STORY

" It happened at Inverkirkaig, Lochinver, one year long ago. After the men folk had gone off to the East Coast fishing, a woman got up one morning to find all the dry-stone-dykes down around her croft. This woman was supposed to be a good friend of his Satanic Majesty, and when asked by a neighbouring woman how she was going to get her dykes lifted again, she said she would find the means. It so happened that in Nedd, near Drumbeg, she had a man friend, who would come and help her; but she had to send her message by asking the devil to communicate with him. This she proceeded to do through a doubtful character in Nedd. When the doubtful one went to

85

deliver the message about the fallen dykes, he found the husband and wife on their knees, and so he was unable to speak to them!"

THE BLACK DOG OF CREAG AN ORDAIN

On the way to Lochinver from Stoer, Sutherland, the dark and gloomy rock of Creag an Ordain overhangs the roadway. It is an eerie spot, and once it used to be haunted by a monster in the shape of a huge black dog. This horrible apparition made itself manifest to foot-travellers, particularly those who had been indulging " Not wisely but too well " in the tavern at Lochinver. The advent of the motor-car proved too much for him and he has apparently abandoned his traditional haunt. However, since then—a mysterious light, known as " The Oldney Light " is frequently seen in the vicinity of Oldney Island.

According to the late Mrs. MacLeod—" The Devil was very real to people in the Stoer district, long ago, and in the days of my own youth, nothing would have induced me to pass gloomy and desolate Loch nan Ordain during the hours of darkness, where the Devil himself was supposed to appear in the form of a large black dog. A relative of mine was one night proceeding along the road which skirts the south-west side of the loch below the high rocks, on the way to Clachtoll, when he heard splashing in the water, and by the light of the waning moon, which came out from behind a cloud, he saw a big, black dog with eyes like glowing peats, emerge from the loch and come straight up the steep bank towards him. He was terrified out of his wits, as the animal growled and spat sparks at him. He fled in terror along the road, the dog following him all the way, until on passing him, it turned round and looked at him, when he beheld a hideous face, human in form, with horns sticking out of its head. As he continued on his way, the dog trotted on in front of him, every now and then looking back at him growling and snarling and belching fire from its grotesque mouth, until all of a sudden, it disappeared through the centre of the highway, giving vent to a diabolical peal of laughter.

My friend was very ill for a long time afterwards, as the result of his encounter with the ' foul fiend.' "

3

WITCHCRAFT

" I heard your scream on the hill-slope; but
I did not pay it heed until I heard the voice of
the raven. A thousand curses on the brothers,
they left before me a mirror, the blood of your
chest, of your mouth and of your throat; and
you lying on the peat-moss."

HIGHLAND CURSE.

Witchcraft and other forms of Diablerie

There is no witchcraft where there is no faith in it;
Cease to believe in it and it will cease to be.—(*Bekker*)

According to Dr. Margaret Murray's definition, a witch
is " anyone who worships a non-Christian god and
claims strange powers to heal or to cast magic spells
for good or evil."

Fairies, mermaids, water-horses and kindred supernatural
beings are distinct from the Evil Spirits that gave to witches
their unhallowed powers. The " beanshithe " and the " each
visge " could not be compelled by mortals to appear when
wanted, or to aid them; the Powers of Darkness, on the other
hand, were always at the service of their votaries, and by means
of charms and incantations known to the initiated might be
made to lend their aid in any nefarious scheme.

Witchcraft was also regarded as the power of magical
incantation through the agency of evil spirits. The superstition
took its rise in the East, and at an early period of the world's
history. Andrew Lang defined Withcraft as " a web of fraud,
folk-medicine and fairy tales "; but it is one of the strangest
and most persistent of Celtic beliefs. It is a combination of
many powers, including a dependence on the Devil. Witches

were believed to work by spells, divination, and the Evil Eye They could transform themselves into the shape of animals especially hares and cats; and by various ways work disaster to man and beast.

The Highland witches, though they once (according to Lindsay) could muster round their prototype of Endor in numerous groups, from

> " Athole and Argyle
> And from Rynnis of Galloway
> With mony wofull walloway."

have now dwindled down to a few old women, deemed " unlucky to meet " by their neighbours.

Though belief in their existence is rapidly dying out, stories of witches and their ways are still told round the peat fire.

A cure for the "Evil Eye"

A cure for the " Evil Eye," as practised in Uist, is as follows:
The person first goes for water, and, if possible, it is taken from a burn across which the living pass, and over which the dead are carried. Having brought the water into the house, he repeats the Paidir (pater) and the Creud (credo). He then takes the coin or coins (the more valuable the more the potency) and, in name of Father, Son and Holy Ghost, puts it or them into the water. Thereafter three palmfuls (tri boiseagan) are sprinkled in name of the Trinity on the person or animal suffering.

The performer then goes with the dish of water to the fireside, and sprinkles three handfuls on the fire, repeating these words :—

> " Will fire burn envy?
> Fire will burn envy."

The remainder of the water is then taken outside, and spilled on a flag or rock—that is, a flag or rock *in situ*. If, after the water is spilled out, and the vessel turned upside down, one or other of the coins adhere to the vessel, always a wooden one, and generally the broth-pot ladle, it is considered proof positive of the need for, and also of the efficacy, of the enchantment.

Storm witches

HOW WITCHES CONTROL THE WEATHER

The Highland Witches are still supposed to control the weather in many parts of the far North, and although belief in their spells is rapidly dying out, stories of witches and their ways are still told round the peat fire. The Gaelic word GEASAN (spell) is still capable of raising a hurricane of sufficient violence to snowbind crofters for days on end.

Although a witch be burned, at death the " geasan " does not die with her. Her dying curse can continue.

There were two famous Storm Witches. One the Storm Witch called Dodyag from Mull, and Morag from Scourie, Sutherland. In fact so potent was the Sutherland witch's spell, that she could not only soothe the waves, but produce terrific snow-storms *at will*.

Local people, today, attribute heavy snow conditions to the " geasan " of Morag.

Morag would sit motionless for hours, all the time crooning a plaintive song. Her aloofness made her the object of suspicion to her neighbours. The old folk knew well that she could foretell disaster to many.

Morag earned a profitable living by selling favourable winds to mariners. Her fee was 6d. and not many masters of vessels would leave the roadstead without paying it to propitiate her. Crofters also consulted her. For this fee she would boil her kettle and give the barque, or the croft, the benefit of her prayers. The wind desired was sure to come, and produced snow-drifts dyke-high, when necessary. Her powers resembled those of a certain King of Sweden, nicknamed Windycap, who was reputed to be so familiar with the evil spirits that, whatever way he turned his cap, the wind would presently blow that way.

Morag would stand, gazing towards the north-west, from which quarter the snow storm was blowing. Slowly, she would raise her staff towards it, and chant a Gaelic invocation, and so soon as her song was ended, the force of the tempest would commence—or abate.

Her hearers, overawed by her tone of menace and reputation of skill in all occult arts, were fully persuaded that the snow-storm was being charmed the way her verse directed it. Her practices, current in the district, were referred to as " whistling to the wind." She could invoke the wind in a shrill, tremendous whistling, looking towards the quarter from which she desired the snow-storm to come.

By waving her hand in the direction opposite to the sweep of the sea, she could also " soothe the waves and the breeze." Morag (Mackay) practised her " geasan " chiefly on the Island of Handa, which lies a little to the northward of Scourie Bay, and is separated from the mainland by the sheltered channel known as Handa Sound.

The clay image

A witch's most efficient way of causing bodily harm to those she hated was by means of the " corp creadh," or clay effigy. An image of the person to be destroyed was made of clay: pins were stuck through it; and it was then placed in a stream of running water. As the water trickled over it and as it was wasted away, so did the person whose effigy it was. This practice was widely spread all over the Highlands. There happens to be a stream near Applecross known as Allt nan Corp (Burn of the Bodies) from the number of clay effigies placed in it for evil purposes of magic. It is on record that in 1590, Catherine Ross (Lady Foulis) and her son-in-law Hector Munro employed the services of a notorious witch to make a clay image of Marjory Campbell, the young wife of Ross of Balnagown, whom Lady Foulis wished to destroy so that she herself might become Lady of Balnagown. They were charged, along with the hag who helped them, with causing sickness to Marjory Campbell by sticking pins and needles into a corp creadh. The witch—

Catherine Ross by name—confessed her guilt before Urquhart of Cromarty and Irvine of Kynnock, and was burned for her crime at Channerie. Lady Foulis and her son-in-law were acquitted. The use of the corp creadh as a love charm is not confined to Celtic witchcraft alone. It dates back to classical times; Virgil describes it.

The three witches of Kintail

A story of Loch Duich, West Ross-shire, as told by Ruraidh Mor, of Ullapool

Long ago, in the village of Kintail on the shores of Loch Duich in West Ross-shire, there lived a ship's carpenter called Willie.

Now Willie's own dinghy needed mending, but neither in his workshop, nor in the village, could he find the right piece of wood. So Willie started off to the woods.

For many hours the carpenter wandered and searched among the pine trees. How long he walked before he realised that he was lost, Willie did not know, but daylight was fading and the woods were wrapped in the damp greyness of the mist.

On and on he went, always, as he thought, in the direction of Kintail. At nearly every step the track became more hazardous and the visibility became worse than ever, until, suddenly, he saw a faint glimmer of light winking through the fog. When he got closer, he found that the light was emanating from a cottage window.

Groping his way to the door, Willie knocked loudly.

From inside there came the sound of shuffling feet. Slowly, the door opened to reveal an old woman; she did not speak, so Willie explained his plight, and only then did she bid him enter. . . .

Now Willie, who had been born and bred in the district and had lived all his life in Kintail, thought it rather strange that he neither recognised the aged lady nor remembered ever having seen the cottage before, and it was with a feeling of wonderment that he followed her into the kitchen, thanking her for her Highland hospitality.

Imagine his surprise when he found that there were two even older ladies seated one at each side of the peat fire. He had never seen them before either.

The first told Willie briefly that the other two were her sisters and, after introducing him, invited the now bewildered carpenter to dine with them, and, since he was very hungry, he accepted gladly and willingly took a dram.

Feeling rather better after the meal, Willie decided to agree to the sisters' suggestion that he should spend the night with them since the mist, which lingered thickly outside, was still pressing against the cottage window.

He was shown to his room—a small one, which contained among other articles of furniture, a bed, a table and chair and a large old-fashioned wooden box opposite the fireplace. The atmosphere of the place felt queer and even sinister. He began to wish that he had never entered this cottage and, for a moment, thought of leaving at once; but he was so tired that he lay down and soon fell asleep.

Willie slept soundly and did not hear the door open, nor did he hear the shuffle of the first sister's slippers as she crossed the room.

He woke with a start only with the creaking of hinges long rusty, and saw her lit by the glow from the smouldering peat fire. She was bending over the old wooden trunk at the foot of his bed, and she looked like a witch. Willie stayed very still and watched. . . .

The old hag searched for a while in the wooden box and then stood up—in her hand she held a small red cap. Carefully she placed it upon her head and slowly she uttered the strangest words: " Here's off to London," she said.

The next moment she had disappeared up " am fàrleus " (the chimney) and Willie lay gasping with surprise and fright.

Hardly had he begun to recover a little when in shuffled the second sister and, going over to the trunk, she too took out a small red bonnet, which she placed on her head, and she, too, lifted her right arm and muttered the same words: " Here's off to London," and immediately vanished after her sister. . .

Not more than a minute later, to his amazement, entered the third sister and she, too, took out a small red cap, and in like manner was spirited away up the chimney. . . .

Willie lay in a state of nervous bewilderment for a while, and wondered what on earth to do.

He pinched himself hard to see if he really was awake and not dreaming these strange happenings. Then he decided the best thing to do would be to get out of bed to search the house. So he crept very quietly out of the bedroom and into the kitchen; but there was no one about and he found on closer investigation that he was entirely alone in the cottage.

Willie returned to the bedroom and decided to have a look inside the trunk. There was nothing inside it but one small red cap. He lifted it out rather carefully and examined it; but it appeared to be a perfectly ordinary bonnet, so he placed it on his head.

And then Willie did a very stupid thing. He was suddenly possessed by a strong feeling of curiosity and, rather timidly, let it be said, he, too, raised his right hand and uttered the words: " Here's off to London! "

No sooner had he done so than, to his astonishment, he immediately found himself walking down Bow Street in London City.

This was the London of Samuel Pepys; the London of coffee and ale houses and cobble stones, and it was into an ale house that Willie turned, and it was strange that he felt no alarm at finding himself in town when all his life had been spent in far-away Scotland; but in he went and imagine his amazement at finding the three old sisters sitting round a table drinking whisky.

They invited him over to join them in a refreshment without showing the slightest surprise.

After the four visitors had consumed their drinks, they sat for a little while watching the men of fashion who drifted in. It seemed to Willie rather strange that they were not astonished to see three such ancient witches sitting in their ale house; but no one appeared to notice anything odd about the Highlanders.

After standing each other a few more drams, the first sister put on the little red cap, which she had taken off on arriving in London, and this time it was her left arm which she raised before she mumbled: " Here's off back to Kintail," and vanished through the smoke-blackened oak beams.

Then the second sister put on her red bonnet and vanished after the first. Then the third sister followed her partners, leaving Willie alone at the table.

He sat there thinking of the mystery of it all, and had also just decided to return to Kintail when a waiter came up to him and presented him with the bill for the drinks.

Of course Willie had no money, so the waiter called in the manager, who sent for the police, and when Willie told them his story, they arrested him at once on a charge of witchcraft.

So poor Willie was flung into prison and eventually he was tried and found guilty—having no feasible defence to offer, and since the penalty for his crime at that time in England was death by hanging, he was sentenced to that fate.

On the day of his execution, the miserable carpenter was removed from his London prison to Hampstead. He was forced on to the scaffold and the rope was fastened about his neck.

" Have you anything to confess? " they asked.

But Willie answered, " No."

" Is there anything you wish to do or say before you meet your doom? " he was asked.

But Willie shook his head; then all of a sudden he had a great idea.

" Yes," said Willie. " I have one small request to make, and it is this: before you hang me, might I put on this small red cap I have in my pocket? "

He was told that there was no reason why he should not, so he carefully put on the red bonnet.

The huge crowd which had gathered to watch his execution saw him raise his left arm and they heard him shout out: " Here's off back to Kintail! " And before their unbelieving gaze he vanished from their sight.

And Willie? Well, he found himself back in his own workshop on the shores of Loch Duich, not only with the rope still round his neck, but with the whole gallows plank as well!

And so there he was back in Kintail with the very piece of wood for which he had been looking for the stem of his boat when he started off on his amazing adventure. It was just exactly what he required to make his boat seaworthy and the rope made a good anchor cord. . . .

In some strange way Willie had great luck in his reconstructed vessel, for he caught more fish on the first occasion he set sail on the loch than had ever been caught before in one day, and to this day the " Miracle of the Fishes " still remains the unsolved mystery of Kintail.

Willie returned to the woods to search for the cottage, but he never found it nor its weird inhabitants—they had completely disappeared. All that remained was his good luck.

So he who wishes to make a good catch of fish on Loch Duich will wear a red cap or have a red " toury " on his Highland bonnet. And you who have heard the legend of Willie the carpenter and the three witches of Kintail know why.

" 'Sann aig ceann an latha a dh'innsear an sgeul."

(The fisherman narrates his tale at the end of his day's fishing.)

The curse of Aultgharrach

In the western part of the parish of Abernethy, in Strathspey, a gurgling brook turns a mill-wheel. This burn is named Aultgharrach (the " rough burn "). It should never be crossed by parties on " matrimonial thoughts intent." It has from time immemorial been the general belief that a crossing under these circumstances would have the most untoward results. Not within the memory of the oldest inhabitant has a marriage party been known to pass this way, with the exception of one luckless couple, who took this course on their wedding day, and who lived to rue their incredulity. This, of course, confirmed in the public mind the validity of the ominous restriction. Tradition says that once upon a time, a certain bridegroom suddenly came to an untimely end at this place. The bride, in her inconsolable agony of heart, forthwith decreed, calling heaven and the powers to witness, that a similar doom might meet any party who, similarly engaged, should take the same course.

The burn, a very small one, is about a mile from Boat-of-Garten. The main road crosses it between Mullingarroch and Street of Kincardine. Not long ago, a huge eel was taken out of the burn. The eel's coils went more than once round the pig's slaughtering tub into which it was placed. The local folk contended that it symbolised " the curse of the Devil! "

As many strange things and misfortunes are alleged to have taken place in the past at this stream, a local farmer confessed to me recently, that he purposely made a four mile detour in order to avoid crossing the Aultgharrach on the eve of his wedding day.

Stein Veg of Tarbert

Stein Veg was an old " wise woman " who lived alone in a solitary cottage on the shores of the Moray Firth. She was reputed to have power over the winds and the waves. A party of fishermen, who were storm-stayed for some days in the neighbourhood, determined to test her magic, and asked her to sell them a favourable wind. Accordingly, one of their number set out to visit her. He found an old, bent, grey-haired hag sitting over a peat-fire in a cottage filling with smoke, which half blinded him and caused his eyes to water. She invited him to sit opposite her, while she threw handfuls of dried seaweed into the blaze, muttering to herself in a strange tongue as she did so. The fisherman made his request for a fair wind, and offered her the money which his companions had contributed to buy it. Grumbling that it was little enough, Stein Veg asked him to bring the water-stoup from his boat.

Marvelling greatly that she knew of its existence, the man did as he was told. When he returned, he found that she had piled the fire high with dry turf. A black cat crouched beside it; and a raven croaked and flapped its wings from the rafters overhead. On the table were bones and a bundle of weeds—all the conventional paraphernalia of the witch. Stein Veg took the water-stoup and told the fisherman to wait outside. He walked towards a mound and sat down, gazing at the house. Suddenly the cottage window flared in the darkness with a strange red light. Shadowy figures passed between the window and the fire. In the darkness, Stein Veg opened the door and called the fisherman over. She gave him the water-stoup, into the mouth of which she had thrust a wisp of straw. " You can sail at dawn," she said, " but take care that you do not remove the wisp of straw until you are safely home." Thankfully, the man grasped the stoup and hurried away from the eerie surroundings of the cottage.

In the morning, the wind fell, and the man and his companions made preparations for setting sail. A gentle wind was blowing from the north-west and the waters of the Firth were calm. The vessel sailed down the Firth. " I wonder," one of the crew remarked, " what the old woman put in that stoup? " The fisherman who had gone to the hag's cottage repeated her warning about not removing the straw; and urged his companions to wait until they were in the shelter of Cromarty Bay before satisfying their curiosity. But the rest of the crew laughed at him, and one man seizing the stoup, pulled out the wisp of straw. There was nothing in the stoup but water. Declaring that Stein Veg was a fraud, he flung the straw into the sea, and emptied the stoup over the side. No sooner had he done so than the sky darkened. The wind veered round suddenly and the sea was lashed into foam. Wave after wave swept over the deck as the boat plunged through the wild sea. The storm raged for twenty-four hours—the fiercest in the Moray Firth in the memory of any living man. The vessel went on to the rocks; and the crew drowned. Only one man lived to tell the tale—the fisherman who bought the favourable wind.

How to raise the wind

A fisherman in the far North-West of Scotland told me about a strange way of raising the wind, believed in chiefly by the people of the Western Islands, and which Caithness fishermen do not like, as it affects their catch of herring.

It seems that when the men leave the Lews for the Caithness fishing in July, some of the women left at home put a number of knots on a woollen thread.

Towards the end of the fishing, or earlier, if they are not successful, they undo these knots one by one, with the result that the wind begins to rise, and the boats not being able to get to sea the hired hands are sent home. They take care not to undo the knots at too great a rate, lest the wind should arise too suddenly, for the loss of the loved ones might in this way be brought about if they happened to be at sea when the last knot is being undone.

A shorter way of making the weather stormy is to draw the cat through the fire—though just how it came to be supposed the poor beast's sufferings could influence the weather would be interesting to know.

The clerical curse of Duthil

Contributed by the courtesy of Ian C. Cameron

Several centuries ago, the superstitious portion of the community of the Scottish Highlands firmly believed that certain individuals were endowed with the gift of prophecy. They also believed that some individuals had the power of blessing and cursing. " Gheibh Baoibh an guidhe gar am faidh an anam trocair " (o wizard women shall obtain their wish should their souls not obtain mercy) is an old saying, and was not even disregarded by some Highlanders less than a hundred years ago.

The Parish of Duthil in Strathspey, had, about the year A.D. 1700, an honest outspoken man as its Minister of Religion. He had, however, not gained that respectful attention on the part of his parishioners which he was entitled to expect in his sacred office. Among the parishioners was a family of con- siderable consequence—the Grants of Dalrachnie—who not only had little respect for religion; but also cared little for the minister. On the other hand, the minister had no respect at all for the Grants and on one occasion, when a son was born in the Grant family, the minister was overheard to remark that another demon was added to the tribe. This unguarded remark reached the ears of the Grants and the offended father determined to avenge the insult.

A great feast and entertainment was organised for the occasion of the baptism of the child. In addition to the neighbours and friends of the Grant family who were invited to the feast, the Grants sent a special invitation to the unsuspecting minister. Quite oblivious to the revengeful designs of his host, the minister was prevailed upon to drink to such an extent that he became no longer responsible for his actions. In this intoxicated state, he retired for the night.

In the morning he awoke much more sober, and to his surprise and shame, he discovered that his host's dairymaid had been his sleeping companion for the night. Whether it was that the Grants persuaded the dairymaid to join the minister when he was asleep, or whether the minister in his intoxicated state prevailed upon her to accompany him when he retired the night before, is not known. However, after this incident, news of which spread like wildfire, the poor clergyman found his position in the community so unbearable, that he soon resigned from his charge.

He left the Parish of Duthil under the impression that the wrong which had been done to him was cruelly premeditated by the Grants, as in fact, it was.

Whilst taking a last look at his beloved parish, he is said to have prayed upon bended knees, that, in order to mark his innocence and avenge the injury which he had sustained, the people of Duthil should be deprived of the services of a godly minister until the seventh generation.

It is doubtful whether the people of Duthil believed that this curse would affect them; but it is a fact that for seven generations the parish was noted for discord in religious matters.

Landmarks formed by witches

On the side of the Croy pool on the River Ardle near Kirkmichael, lies a huge stone said to have been dropped by a Glen Shee witch.

An old witch—" one-eyed, with a blue-black face and hair like frosted twigs " was said to be responsible for the tumbled mountains of Ross-shire. Ben Wyvis and Little Wyvis were formed by rocks accidentally dropped from her apron as she sailed through the clouds overhead.

Two large boulders—one on each side of the Kyle of Durness, Sutherland—are connected in local tradition with two witches who lived one on either side of the Kyle. Both were very strong and they frequently quarrelled as to which was the stronger. In order to settle the matter, they decided to have a competition in throwing each a stone of equal size and weight. It was arranged they should throw the stones across the Kyle when the tide was in, and the one who threw hers furthest above high-water-mark would be the winner. One stone landed within a few feet of the west shore; the other fully a hundred yards above high-water-mark on the east side. There they remain to this day.

There are many other similar stories connected with boulders throughout the Scottish Highlands in which mighty stones are pointed out by the local folk to this present time, as evidence of the tremendous strength of these winged spirits of the Devil.

Earl Beardie

One of the traditional rhymes of Angus tells us that—
" When Finhaven Castle runs to sand
The world's end is near at hand."

The castle referred to—former seat of the Crawford family and some miles north-east of Forfar—is still a substantial ruin, showing no signs of fulfilling the prophecy for some considerable time. Finhaven Castle was the home of Alexander, Earl of Crawford, notorious in Scottish history for his rebellion against James II, and known as The Tiger Earl or Earl Beardie. He terrified the country people by his cruelty and acts of aggression.

A messenger once cut a cudgel from a Spanish chestnut tree in the grounds of Finhaven Castle, and Earl Beardie hanged him for the offence on one of its boughs: but the ghost of the luckless man still " walks " between Finhaven and Cariston; and a local rhyme says that—

" Earl Beardie never will dee
Nor puir Jock Barefoot be set free
As lang's there grows a chestnut tree."

The remarkable opening statement of this verse refers to the following legend:—Earl Beardie was an inveterate gambler; and one night he was playing cards at Glamis and was losing heavily. The then Earl of Glamis advised him to stop play ng; but he swore in his rage that he would go on playing until the day of judgment. As he spoke, there came a clap of thunder and a flash of lightning, and the Devil himself appeared in the room; and the room and all the people in it disappeared for ever from mortal sight. According to local tradition, Earl Beardie and his friends are still playing cards in the " secret chamber " at Glamis and will go on until the crack of Doom!

The witch of Strathardle

The Witches' Garnet Stone of Strathardle was presented to me by an old worthy of the Parish of Kirkmichael, Perthshire, named Jock Fell (" The Sailor ") some years before his death, and the following legend concerning this stone was told to me by him:—

Many years ago, a young man named Robert Wallace, son of a crofter, lived in a small cottage at the foot of a steep hill on the Kirkmichael-Glenshee road below Tonloid, near a ford (now spanned by a stone bridge) on the Allt Menach— locally known as the Dunie Burn, fell in love with a beautiful girl called Christina Rattray who lived in the village of Kirkmichael. Her cousin—Jessie Cameron, who was also in love with Robert Wallace, and who was supposed to possess " The Black Art " (a gift from a Glenshee witch)—conceived an ill-will towards Christina and made a Corp Chre, or Corp Chreadh (clay image or body) as a means of effecting the destruction of her cousin. Robbie preferred the prettier of the girls; but the

102

other loved him so much that she determined to destroy her rival. So Jessie made the Corp of clay resemble Christina's human body and stuck pins in it, and with every pin inserted, she pronounced an incantation.

To ensure that Christina should die a lingering death, Jessie took care to see that the pins should not touch the area where the heart was supposed to be. She then carried the Corp to the Dunie Burn, one night, and placed it in the running stream near the usual trysting place, where the burn rushes down a glacier rut for about eighty yards. There is a small waterfall at the head of the channel through which the burn gushes, and this particular stretch of stream is locally known to this day as the Witches' Pool. The Corp was made as hard as possible at first; but when Jessie placed it in the pool, by-and-by, the current began to wear it away. And as it crumbled under the force of the water, so did the person represented begin to become weak and lean, and at last became so ill that she had to take to her bed. At the same time, it was observed that a change had come over Jessie, and that her hitherto sweet nature had changed. She was sullen and nervous in temperament and disinclined to mix in company. The attentions of the lover, her friends, or the doctor failed to restore Christina to health.

About this time a shepherd in the locality, crossing the Dunie Burn in search of a strayed sheep, noticed the Corp Chre in the water. He said to himself: " This is nothing but the work of Satan; so taking it out of the stream, he destroyed it. On reaching home, he informed his mother of what he had seen. The old woman at once remarked: " It is just the work of Satan; some wicked person has done that to destroy our neighbour's beautiful daughter. Say nothing to anyone about it and you will see she will soon recover." The mother of the shepherd then went to see the sick girl and told her what had been done. The girl had become very weak and was considered to be near her end; but from the day the shepherd had destroyed the clay figure she improved in health steadily. The jealous girl, at a loss to understand how her scheme had failed, went to ask for the sick one. On entering the cottage she said: " You are getting better? "

" Yes," was the answer, " in His name, I am."

The wicked girl went away, and on going to the burn where she had placed the figure, she saw that it had been destroyed. She set about making another; but suspicion having been awakened, she was watched, and being caught making it, she was seized and tried for witchcraft, and found guilty; but as she refused to confess her guilt and pled for mercy, it was decided that she should undergo a certain test by which she might prove her innocence. She was dragged to the Dunie Burn, bound hand and foot and secured by a chain to an iron ring firmly embedded in the garnet rock of the Witches' Pool, and completely immersed in the water. Should she survive the ordeal over night, her innocence would be proved. As she sank into the icy depths, she solemnly chanted a Gaelic invocation to the Witch of Glenshee. Suddenly, a raven alighted on the topmost ledge of rock and a great black storm-wrack cloud obscured the tree-tops, followed by a gale. That night a tremendous thunderstorm burst forth over the strath—believed to have been the fiercest on record—one peal of thunder alone, it is said, reverberated amongst the hills for over an hour's duration. Over and above the roar of the thunder and the noise of the tempest, the fiendish snarls of the infuriated Glenshee witch, who was supposed to have power over storms, echoed through the darkness. In the morning, it was found that one of the vivid flashes of fork-lightning had split the garnet stone into fragments, and no trace of Jessie Cameron could be found in the swollen waters of the Dunie Burn—nor has any trace of her body been found to this day.

Apparently the Glenshee witch had successfully rescued her prototype and conveyed her away to the heights of Mount Blair. To this day, the hill road leading down to the Dunie Burn is known as " Robbie Wallace's Brae."

The witch of Laggan

A Badenoch hunter who persecuted all witches was once caught in a storm and took shelter in a rude hut on the mountainside. A black cat entered the hut, and the hunter had great difficulty in pacifying his dogs. When the cat saw this, it spoke to the hunter, saying: " I am a witch and have taken on this shape; but if you give me shelter, I will cease my wicked ways." The man took pity on the cat with the human voice, and motioned it to sit by the fire. " Not unless you tie up your dogs with a rope," he was told. He then took the hounds to a corner of the hut; but cunningly wound the rope round a beam. Then the cat changed its shape suddenly to that of " the wife of Laggan," and telling the hunter that because he was a persecutor of witches, his hour had come, she flew at his throat. The dogs strained at the rope, the beam cracked, and they were free in an instant. The witch tried to escape, but the dogs worried her as long as they were able. Eventually she did escape from their fangs. When the hunter reached home, his wife told him that she had been visiting " the Wife of Laggan," the reputed witch, who lay ill. This confirmed his suspicions, and when he reached the cottage where the old woman lay, he saw that she was dying of the terrible throat wounds inflicted by his dogs. That night, two men met a woman running in the direction of the churchyard, blood streaming from her throat, and two black dogs at her heels. Close behind followed a man on a black horse. This little procession passed them so quickly that they were doubting the evidence of their eyes, when they saw the horseman returning, with the woman lying dead on the saddle in front of him. Horse and rider disappeared from view in a dark mist.

" Dòmhnull Dubh " himself, the Prince of Darkness, had come to claim his votaress before she could reach consecrated ground on which to die. So passed the Witch of Laggan.

" Treasure Island "
TOBERMORY ARGOSY
As told to me by a native of Mull

Following the defeat of the Spanish Armada in July, 1588, some of the Spanish ships, in an attempt to escape, sailed towards the North of Scotland. Satisfied that the enemy could make no Scottish port, the English left off the pursuit on 20th August, by which time the Armada was roughly a hundred miles east of the Firth of Forth.

After the English vessels had disappeared beyond the horizon, the Spaniards decided to sail round Orkney and then far enough out into the Atlantic to allow them to strike a straight course for Spain.

One of the galleons was the treasure-ship " Florencia " or " Florida " (of 56 guns and some 30,000,000 of money, together with other ornaments, munitions and goods thought to be of great value) which on account of a great storm sought shelter in the Sound of Mull off Tobermory. The curious Mull folk gathered from all over the island to see the ship and numerous sight-seers rowed alongside daily and many were allowed to board it, including MacLean, the Chief of Duart.

As supplies of food began to run short, Don Fareija, commander of the " Florida," demanded that MacLean should supply him with provisions; but MacLean replied that it was not the custom for the chief of MacLean to return hospitality to a menacing alien. However MacLean finally agreed, on the understanding that Don Fareija would pay for what he got, and lend him a hundred men from his crew.

About that time, Lachlan Mòr MacLean of Duart's widowed mother had just been married at Torloisk to MacIan of Ardnamurchan; but on the night of the wedding, his whole retinue were murdered when attending the festivities, with the exception of two, and the bridegroom was spared but imprisoned.

Lachlan enlisted the hundred Spaniards to raid MacIan's lands and the crew " ravaged and plundered the islands of Rum, Eigg, Canna and Muck, burning the inhabitants without respect for age or sex " and the services of the Spaniards were of some avail.

Some time afterwards, the Spanish commander recalled his sailors to the " Florida " and one of the Clan sent word to MacLean that the Spaniards intended to set sail from the Sound of Mull without paying for the provisions supplied. MacLean returned the company of Spaniards to the galleon under the charge of Donald Glas, son of John Dubh MacLean of Morven, whom he entrusted with the duty of collecting the payment due; but he detained three of the principal officers as hostages.

As soon as Donald Glas boarded the " Florida," he was made prisoner and the Spaniards made ready for immediate departure. Out of revenge Donald Glas, finding a favourable opportunity, set fire to the powder magazine and blew the ship up.

Only three out of the 300 Spaniards on board survived, one of them dying the next day, and according to local legend, none but the mermaids know where the treasure lies " fathoms deep beneath the wave."

The Spanish officers who were held by the Chief of MacLean, were at once liberated, when they proceeded immediately to Edinburgh where they tendered a complaint against MacLean who, they contended, was responsible for the destruction of their galleon.

The Mull Storm-Witches

When the news reached Spain about the disaster, vengeance was vowed against the people of Mull and one named Captain Forast was sent in a brigantine to the island to destroy the inhabitants. But when the men of Mull observed the Spanish vessel, they sought out a storm-witch called Dodyag (who shunned her neighbours and scarcely ever left her croft) and promised her much gold if she would by her ' geasan ' (spells) raise a hurricane of sufficient violence to sink the galleass which had anchored in Loch Duan.

Dodyag was supposed to have power over storms and could chant her plaintive melodies to lure the Storm King from his caverns of the deep. Thus she had earned the title of the Storm Witch. This bent hag, with grey hair and flashing eyes appeared before her superstitious beholders as a veritable sorceress, wearing a black coat over a crimson petticoat with mysterious emblems imprinted thereon, and looking in the direction of the breeze with divining staff in hand, she solemnly chanted a " Gaelic " invocation.

As the Spaniards were preparing to land, a strong gale arose and the superstitious knew that Dodyag had foretold disaster to the crew, and said she could only have gained her Black Art through intercourse with the Evil One. But the people believed that the Spanish Captain was himself skilled in witchcraft. So Dodyag transformed herself into the likeness of a raven and flew all over the country to collect eleven other Argyll witches— who also in the semblance of ravens, alighted on the top-mast of the ship. Captain Forast, however, was so powerful in the Black Art that he believed he could outwit all the twelve witches. But Dodyag then sought Big Gormla, a terrible sorceress from Lochaber, to help them. Her hearers overawed by her tone of menace, were fully persuaded that the gale was now being charmed into a raging tornado, as she joined in her incantations.

As Captain Forast was battling with the whirlwind, he observed a great black storm-wrack of cloud obscure the crow's-nest, above which the ravens had perched, and realised that his doom was sealed. For two days, the ship's anchors held out against the tempest; but on the third night, the wind was so strong that some of the cables parted, and the hulk drifted helplessly before the storm until she struck on the King's Point in Morven across the Sound.

The galleon was completely wrecked and all on her perished!

The Athole witches

The sixteenth and seventeenth centuries were troublous and unsettled in Athole—a period of sieges and feuds, and of strife between the Strathardle lairds and the Earls of Athole. This was the golden age of witchcraft and witches and sorcerers undaunted by severe laws against the practising of the Black Art, by the witch-trials and subsequent tortures, were swarming in Athole. They had a great power over commons and nobles alike, and gleaned rich rewards from their nefarious trade. They were in the habit of holding frequent councils, said to be presided over by the Devil himself; and the strength of the movement may be gauged by the recorded fact that at one such conventicle, held in 1597, there were no fewer than 2,300 witches assembled. The Athole witches took a great interest in affairs of State, and even took sides in disputes about succession, etc. " All the witches of Athole " held a meeting in favour of Queen Mary, after which they presented her with a gold-covered deer horn in token of their friendship. After the manner of Shakespeare's " weird sisters " with their " All hail, Macbeth, that shall be king hereafter! " the horn was engraved with emblems prophetic of Mary's sure triumph over all her enemies —the thistle of Scotland superimposed on the rose of England, the figure of a crowned queen on a throne, and an engraving of a large lion with its paw on the face of a smaller one, with the rhyme—

" Fall what may fall,
The lion shall be lord of all."

Unhappily for Mary, however—and for the reputation of the Athole witches—their prophecy did not come to pass.

The Devil at Conon

Near Conon House, in Ross-shire, is an old churchyard on the bank of the River Conon, dedicated in the sixth century A.D. to St. Bride of Kildare. At one time there stood a chapel likewise dedicated to St. Bride, but only the site now remains. According to a local story, concerning a mysterious death in this chapel: One autumn day several hundred years ago while harvesters of Lag a'Bhile (a small hamlet which stood on the site of the present Conon House) were reaping in Pairc na h-eaglaise (Church-field) they saw a man making for the ford in great haste. Believing that he was about to drown himself, they seized hold of him and managed to elicit from him the fact that many years previously he had sold himself to the Devil, and that in fulfilment of this bond he had that day at noon to deliver himself up to his master at the ford.

The harvesters were determined to save him, and carried him, despite his struggles, to the chapel, where they shut him in, leaving him, as they hoped, safely under the protection of " Sweet St. Bride of yellow, yellow hair." Shortly afterwards, at the mid-day hour, a tall dark figure was seen to materialise by the ford, and an unearthly voice was heard crying: " The hour has come but not the man! The hour has come, but not the man !" So saying the figure disappeared. Late that evening when they considered that the fatal hour was sufficiently long past, the harvesters went into the chapel to release the wretched man. They found him dead, with his face under the water of the font. He had kept his vow, and the Devil had claimed his own.

The Devil's gift

" The Red Book of Appin "

The Red Book of Appin was said to have been a gift from the Devil.

The story is of a miller at Bearachan, on Loch Awe side, who was renowned for his uncontrollable temper.

This miller had an apprentice whom he frequently overworked and bullied. Late one night as the youth was in the act of finishing work, a tall dark stranger entered the mill and spoke sympathetically to him, promising to pay him higher wages than the miller did and to treat him kindly if he consented to work for him. The stranger arranged to meet the lad on a certain night at Cama-linn on Monadh Meadhonach (the Middle Mountain). The apprentice, however, became frightened, and the following day confessed to his master about his visitor.

A conclave of sixteen ministers was called. They decided that the lad should keep the appointment; but advised him to cut a branch from a rowan tree and take the wand with him, and when he should reach the trysting place to draw a circle with it round himself, out of which he should not move, no matter what the stranger should say or do. A band of them went to watch the meeting from a neighbouring hill.

At the appointed hour, the dark stranger appeared, and before handing over the promised money, asked the boy to write his name in a red book, which he threw over to him. Once the apprentice had the book in his possession, he refused to give it up. The Demon then showed himself in his true colours. First he transformed himself into a mial chu riabhach (a grizzled grey-hound), and dashed madly against the magic circle; then into a roaring bull; then into a flock of crows, which wheeled and swooped above the terrified lad, trying with the wind raised by their wings to lift him out of his haven of refuge. This continued until a cock crew, when the Devil abandoned his efforts and disappeared.

The book which the boy retained became " The Red Book of Appin," which was said to contain charms for the cure of disease of cattle—so powerful that its owner had to encircle his head with an iron hoop every time he opened it. The Red Book of Appin was last known to be in the possession of the Stewarts of Invernehyle.

The Comyn and the witch of Badenoch

At the foot of Glen Fernate, in Strathardle, is an immense boulder known as Clach Mòr. It stands twenty feet above the ground, is seventy-four feet in circumference, and weighs nearly one thousand tons. It is a different kind of stone from any of the other rocks found in the neighbourhood, and the scientific explanation of its presence in Glen Fernate is that in the early glacial ages of the world, it must have floated to Scotland from a distant land, embedded in an iceberg, and been stranded there. But tradition vies with science in explaining the presence of the Big Stone, and attributes it to the doings of a witch.

According to the legend, when the Cummings, long centuries ago, were Lords of Badenoch, the great Comyn wished to build a castle there so strong that no human hands could capture it; so instead of employing masons to erect it, he engaged the services of a notorious Badenoch witch who, in return for much gold, agreed to carry stones in her apron and to build an impreg-nable castle.

First of all, she began a search for two huge boulders of equal size and shape for door-posts for the outer gate; but could not find two such matching stones in the whole of Scotland. She was in despair until on one of her nocturnal excursions she met a sister witch from the Isle of Man—at that time famous as a stronghold of the Devil—who told her of two enormous twin stones on the Manx hills.

The next night, she started off for the Isle of Man just after sunset, and left for Badenoch again with one of the stones when the countryside was bathed in bright moonlight. As dawn broke, she was passing the head of Glen Fernate on her homeward journey, just as a hunter was coming from the Athole Forest with a deer on his back. Seeing the great black mass come flying through the air, he exclaimed, " Dhia gleidh mise! " (God preserve me!). . . .

The utterance of the Holy Name broke the witch's power; her apron-string snapped in two, and the stone rolled down to the bottom of Glen Fernate, where it lies to this day. She could never get another apron-string which would bear even lighter stones, and the Comyn's castle was never built. It is said that on each anniversary of that night the witch returns, and labours from sunset to sunrise trying to move the Clach Mòr, and that some of the older local people give the uncanny spot a wide berth after dark.

Witch Mabel

One bright summer day in the month of June many years ago, a farmer's wife in Orkney noticed a peculiar object beside her cow. She called to her husband and son to come out and see what it was. On approaching the grass plot where the animal was grazing, they saw to their great astonishment a large hare milking the cow!

As soon as the hare sighted them it leapt away over the grass. The two men, calling to their dog, set out after it, and hunted it for a few miles till they saw it disappear through the open door of a mountain cottage. They also entered and found an old woman lying on the hearth in front of the peat-fire, panting for breath. Her clothes were covered with mud.

They did not wait to see more, but ran out of the cottage in fear, and spread the report throughout the neighbourhood that old Mabel of the brae-head was a witch. In those superstitious days, such a story required no second telling to be believed, and soon every village in the district was up in arms against the supposed witch.

Mabel was seized and carried to the Gallowhill of Kirkwall, where a pyre was kindled. There she was tied to the stake and burned to death. Her ashes, we are told, " were afterwards collected and scattered to the four winds of heaven."

The Devil and his agents

According to a paper by Dr. Alex. McBain in Transactions of Gaelic Society of Inverness for the year 1888, " The Devil is apt to be cheated by clever mortals. He had in former times a black school or " sgoil dhubh " in Italy, where some adventurous Highlanders went and received training in " the art that none man name." At the end of the session or period of training the pupils were all set free at once out of a dark room, and the Devil stood at the door to seize the last man as they rushed out, for the last man was his due. The clever Gael cheated the Devil easily. As he came up leisurely, his majesty made a grab at him, but the scholar objected, declaring that there was one behind him, and pointing to his shadow. The Devil then seized the shadow and the substantial man escaped, but was ever after shadowless. In Sutherlandshire the hero of this tale is one of the Reay Chiefs called Donald Duival Mackay, said to be the first Baron Reay, 1628. Elsewhere Michael Scott is the hero of these stories."

That the Devil could appear to men and enter into unholy compacts with them, is a very ancient belief. He was regarded as the master of all witches and magicians, who on stated occasions assembled and did homage to him.

The Devil could assume many shapes, human and animal. If he assumed the form of a human being, he was generally seen as a dark, handsome stranger (easily recognised, however, by having hoofs instead of feet). The animal shapes he affected most were those of a dog or a horse, usually black.

The Devil might be cheated by clever mortals who had mastered the " Sgoil dubh Shatain " (Black Art); and he could be propitiated; but most often he succeeded in his nefarious schemes.

In addition to his Scriptural titles, the Devil is known in Gaelic as Am fear nach abair mi (The one whom I will not mention); An t-aibhirteir (The one from the abyss); An riabhach mòr (The big grizzled one). The most common name, however, is Dòmhnull Dubh (Black Donald).

Satan's agents, who were capable of paying not only proper attention to their own private affairs, but likewise of carrying on almost all business of the Evil One in this land, were at one time unaccountably active in the North. They were endowed with ample powers of transmigration, consequently there was no similitude from their own proper likenesses to that of a cat or a stone, but they could assume at pleasure. Hence the speed and privacy with which they were able to attain their evil ends. One of the most ordinary disguises of a " Bana-Bhuidseach " is the similitude of a hare—an exceedingly convenient transformation while in the field, executing undertakings with great expedition and to escape fleetly on any emergency. A likeness of a cat, procured admission to the innermost recesses of a dwelling, to deposit infernal machinery, without exciting suspicion. A third guise, was the transformation into a stone—a common practice with the witch in the season of agricultural operations, by which great opportunities were afforded of mischief to the farmer's interest. The wily witch would penetrate into the ground, and place herself in the line of a plough and, as it passed her, she would creep in betwixt the cock and the culter. The plough was in consequence expelled from the ground for a considerable space. A fourth, was her transformation into the shape of a raven to attend the counsels of Satan. The witch likewise might assume the character of a magpie on occasions of sudden emergency, to avoid suspicion.

According to a Fodderty authority: " I have frequently gone to the burn for ' pourn arigid,' but always under a severe exhortation not to open my mouth to speak to any person until my return; if I were to do so, the spell would not operate.

When no gold coin was available, I have seen the wedding-ring used instead, along with a shilling and a halfpenny."

EDITOR'S NOTE:

In Vol. XVIII of the Inverness Gaelic Society's Transactions, there is a long and interesting paper on the above subject, by Mr. William Mackenzie, at one time Secretary to the Crofters' Commission, who made a special study of the "Evil Eye" among the people of the West Coast.

The Devil described

The late Angus Morrison, a native of Sheigra, near Kinlochbervie, in Sutherland, gave this account of a fearful experience on a winter night, while on the way home to his croft at the road end. When I interviewed him outside his croft he said: "The Devil never walks on the highway. He is not allowed to do so. He is always encountered at the side of the road: So, you can always be certain it is the Devil, if you should see him standing at the road-side. One December night, some years ago, I was walking home from Oldshore More in the darkness in company with a friend. As we left Balchrick and rounded a bend in the road below the high rocks, we saw a great brute of a man seemingly the size of a telegraph pole. My friend fled in terror, leaving me alone. I was shaking all over, too afraid to move. I knew it was the Devil. He was standing at the edge of the highway beside a ditch which runs the length of the road at that part. He had a white front (or waistcoat), but otherwise he was dressed in black. I could not see his face very clearly; but I did see that sparks were coming out of his nose and mouth. I was speechless. I felt as if my clothes were taken off. I could not move from where I stood. The thing was horrible. It was the Devil, sure enough; he was black and thick. He was a rascal! Yes, about the size of a ship's mast. I clearly saw him for about two minutes before he suddenly took it into his head to walk away in the direction of the sea. I could hear the sound of his hoofbeats.

My friend was waiting for me along the road, and after he saw me home, I felt faint. I was ill for many days afterwards, wondering if the thing would come to my croft; but he never paid me a visit."

Angus Morrison spoke mostly in Gaelic, and being a very old man, and not a clear speaker, I had difficulty in writing down all he said.

Mr. Morrison, who was then in his 91st year, was a respected tenant on the Kinlochbervie Estate. He was full of stories and legends concerning ghosts, devils, fairies, mermaids, monsters and witches. A most interesting and kindly man, he wore one gold earing. He died in the autumn of 1956.

The witch of Monzie

Behind the wooded " Knock " of Crieff, in Perthshire, some distance above the main road that goes from Gilmerton up towards the Sma' Glen, lies the quiet little village of Monzie, the name of which became famous (or infamous) during the eighteenth century by reason of its connection with Kate McNiven, the " Witch of Monzie." This old woman lived in a small cottage on the right bank of the Shaggie Burn, and at times she was employed as a nurse at the house of Inchbrackie, some miles to the south-east. Tradition has it that the Laird of Inchbrackie was one of the first to have practical experience of Kate's powers of " buidseachd " (sorcery). He rode over one day on business to Dunning, taking with him (as was the custom in these days) his own silver knife and fork. While seated at dinner he was annoyed by a large bee which buzzed persistently round his head, and at last in a rage threw down knife and fork and beat off the insect, which flew buzzing out of the window. When the laird resumed his seat, he found to his astonishment that his knife and fork had disappeared! On returning to Inchbrackie, he related his strange experience; and shortly afterwards (so the story goes), the missing cutlery was found in the possession of the Witch of Monzie.

Now that the specific crime of theft was laid to her charge, former mysterious incidents were brought up against her; and a campaign against witchcraft was not long in spreading. Early in 1715 she was apprehended, tried and condemned to be burned. The burning took place at a part of the Knock which to this day is known as " Kate McNiven's Crag." Her last hours are said to have been accompanied by scenes usual to witch-burnings, a lurid confession of past misdeeds and a parting curse—which in her case took the form of malediction on the Lairds of Monzie, that their line should never have a lineal successor; and on the parish Minister (possibly because of his pulpit tirades against witchcraft and superstition), that ill-luck should attend him and his successors for ever.

According to the legend, the Laird of Inchbrackie made a last-minute intercession (in vain) on Kate's behalf, and was rewarded by the gift of a bluish stone, like an uncut sapphire, which she gave him as she died, with the prophecy that so long as it was retained by his family, they would never lack heirs. " And it must be admitted," writes Hamish Miles, who also tells this story in his book " Fair Perthshire "—" that they did not ! "

The witch and the warlock

On the south bank of the Dee, forming part of the background of the Castle of Abergeldie, is a hill called Craig nam Ban (The Rock of the Women), associated in popular tradition with the burning of the last witch in the district. The date of the occurrence is rather indefinite; but the story goes that when witches were rampant all over Scotland and honest people burned as many of them as they could convict, a " cailleach " who lived near the Dee was accused of practising withcraft and was condemned to die. An old man who had associated himself with many of her malpractices was put into confinement with her. One dark night the witch succeeded in making her escape, and the warlock undertook to bring her back, on condition that he would receive a free pardon. He had not travelled very far in search of her, when he saw a hare, which he knew to be his

117

quarry under another form. Changing himself into a greyhound, he gave chase; but as he was about to seize the smaller animal, it took the form of a mouse and ran into a crevice of a dyke. At once the greyhound assumed the form of a weasel and, darting into the hole, brought out the mouse. The two then assumed human shape, and the old woman was delivered up to her enemies and burned on the top of Carn nam Ban.

Maclean and the evil one

A story told by the late Mr. Euan Macdiarmid, C.A.,
Edinburgh

There was a hill called " Grogan " near Aberfeldy, beside the farm of Auchbane. Robert Maclean, the farmer, had his whisky-still concealed in a cave on the hillside, and spent too much of his time on this illicit business. He was occupied with his whisky making one Sabbath morning when suddenly there was a thunderous knock on the door. " Co an diabhol rinn sin? " (Who the Devil did that?) shouted Maclean. There entered a tall swarthy stranger attired in a frock coat and white trousers, who said, " You mentioned my name just now, and here I am. You will meet me tomorrow at midnight on Grandtully Hill." Having said this, the stranger vanished. Maclean stood shaking and aghast. Next night he met the stranger at the appointed place, and they wrestled for hours. These ghastly encounters took place night after night, and Maclean became worn to a shadow. Also, he was so saturated with satanic influence that his own horses shied and bit at him whenever he went near them, and his cat with its back arched and his dog with unearthly howls fled from the house. His relatives were worried about his condition, and called in the minister of Weem, who diagnosed that Maclean was suffering from the influence of the Evil One. He instructed him to carry a Bible and a broadsword to the next encounter. With the broadsword he was to describe a circle round himself, and then with his Bible and sword raised aloft he was to defy the Evil One to come and do his worst. This display proved too much for the Devil and Maclean was at last rid of his oppressor. But he was now a chastened man, and thereafter was an industrious farmer and a regular churchgoer.

Taghairm

THE DEVIL'S SUPPER

This Ceremony may be still held in certain parts of Argyll and the Inner Hebrides, including the isles of Mull and Islay. The late Mr. James MacKillop, Factor, Islay House, told me how he had witnessed " Taghairm " with disgust

TAGHAIRM was the name given to the repulsive ceremony known as " Giving supper to the Devil." The Ceremony itself falls under the category of witchcraft. It takes the form of roasting cats alive on spits until Dòmhnuil Dubh himself appears in the shape of a cat. When this happens, the Devil is compelled to grant whatever wish the perpetrators of the cruel deed might seek.

Two men of Pennygown in Mull, are said to have performed a similar ceremony in days past. They roasted cats alive on spits over a blazing fire inside a barn. The death shrieks of the tortured creatures attracted others of their kind, until the barn became a perfect inferno of cats. As each beast entered the building it said—" 'S olc an càramh cat sin " (This is ill-usage for a cat), to which their torturers replied that it would be better shortly.

At last, just as the men were expecting to be torn to pieces by the infuriated animals, a huge black cat appeared, causing all the other cats which had assembled, to be silent. One of the executioners struck the newcomer a mighty blow on the head with a claymore, and under the potent spell of " Taghairm," the Devil assumed his proper shape and asked the summoners what they wanted with him. They demanded—" Cuid 'us conach, 'us saoghal fada na cheann " (Property and prosperity, and a long life to enjoy it).

The Devil rushed out of the door crying—" Conach! Conach! Conach! (Prosperity! Prosperity! Prosperity!). The wish was granted; but according to the legend, the men were obliged to repeat the " Taghairm " every year in order to keep the Devil to his promise.

4

MONSTERS

" I saw the monsters . . . go heaving by; the
long lithe beasts that are toothed to their tails."

(JAMES STEPHENS)

Monsters

Stories of Monsters, said the late John Gregorson Campbell,
" depend not so much on the imagination of the individual
spectator as on accumulated rumours; and their explanation is to be sought in men's love of the marvellous, and ten-
dency to exaggeration." A rock by the side of a loch, looming
up in the darkness; a pine tree swayed by the wind; an upturned
boat on the shore; a fog-bank stretching out to sea in the grey
dawn—all might easily be mistaken for strange creatures hostile
to man; and once this belief became popular, fear and rumour
would do the rest.

The early tales concerning monsters and water-horses
belong to the region of folk-lore rather than fiction, and appear
with comparatively little variation in the traditions of all
countries, with the exception of the Scottish Highlands; where
stories of the weird differ considerably. There the hauntings
are real hauntings and monsters and kelpies, not to mention
ghosts and " seers " actually exist to this day in the lonely
horror of dark places.

The water-horse myth in Celtic mythology is rather a curious
notion. This creature was entirely a stranger to the fauna of
not only Britain but Europe and, although not always so, must
have been ages before the first Celtic migration—probably
before the appearance of anthropoidal man himself.

When we consider how improbable it is that the Celt should
know of such an animal having pre-existed him, we wonder
how the Celt derived his knowledge of the water-horse cult.
Did the Celt bring it with him from his Eastern home, and in

the course of ages did that which was a reality degenerate into that which is mythical?

The " cirein croin " (Sea-serpent) was believed by High-landers and Islanders alike to be the largest animal in the world. They called it " mial mhòr a chuain " (great beast of the ocean) and " cuartag mhòr a chuain " (great whirlpool of the ocean).

Sea serpents have frequently been seen round our Scottish coasts; but often enough they have been confused with conger eels. The men of Loch Awe were supposed to have been afraid of the eels of Loch Edive (Etive) which were reputed to be " as big as ane horse with ane certain incredible length."

In August, 1872, a sea serpent was observed in the Sound of Sleat, between Skye and the mainland, by the Rev. John Macrae of Glenelg and a clerical friend. They described it as a humped creature about 45 feet in length, black in colour, with a small, flat head. Twenty years later, a similar creature appeared in Loch Alsh, and was described by a London doctor who saw it, as brown in colour, and shining, with a giraffe-like neck.

In 1919, a long-necked sea-creature, with a head " like a black or dark brown retriever, with small beady black eyes " was seen in the Pentland Firth.

In 1931, Dr. John Paton of Langside, Glasgow, was cycling with his daughter in the Island of Arran when they saw in the water what looked like an up-turned boat. To their amazement, the object reared a " parrot-like " beaked head, then seemingly took fright and floundered off its rock into the sea. " I am familiar with seals, sharks, whales, etc.," wrote Dr. Paton, " and what I saw was unique." He described the creature as " longer than an elephant " and greenish-brown in colour, with a serrated tail and a mane like that of a horse.

A report of another sea serpent came from two Fife fishermen, who on 4th July, 1939, reported having observed one in the Firth of Forth. They described it as having a head and neck like that of a horse, protruding eyes, and a dark brown smooth, ratlike skin. The men were fishing about 400 yards off the shore east of Wemyss, when they sighted the creature. They sailed round it for nearly an hour, during which time it stared warily at them, diving under water whenever they approached too closely. One of the men, who had had experience of deep-sea fishing in many waters, said that what he saw was no known species of sea-creature. " Its head," he reported, " was between that of a horse, and a bear. Its neck was like that of a horse, and when the neck was shot upright out of the water the head was about three feet above the surface."

The Loch Ness monster

Loch Ness is often referred to as the " Queer Loch " on account of the legends regarding its monster, which through ages is supposed to have disported itself on the surface of the water on calm days. In fact, there seems to be more in the monster story of Loch Ness than mere imagination.

In *The Life of St. Columba* a " great beast " is described in the river Ness. As St. Columba lived in the early part of the sixth century, this means that the Loch Ness Monster is probably fourteen centuries old !

The ninth Abbot, Adamnan, in his book on St. Columba, written in A.D. 670, tells how the Saint was once crossing the river Ness when he saw some of the inhabitants burying an unfortunate man who had been seized while swimming by the monster, and so horribly mutilated that he was dead before his friends could pull him out of the water. St. Columba, on hearing this, ordered one of his companions to swim across the Loch. He did so, and the monster, scenting further prey, rose again to the surface. The holy man then raised his right hand, and making the Sign of the Cross in the air, invoked the monster in the name of God to " go with all speed." The beast was so terrified at the voice of the Saint that it sank instantaneously to its lair, and the swimmer returned unharmed to the shore.

Another legend, of later years, tells how a tinker and his dog took refuge one cold autumn night in a cave in the rocks below Abriachan on the shores of the loch. As the wind was chill, the tinker placed some pieces of brushwood across the mouth of the cavern in order to seal his humble dwelling from the icy blast. After cooking his supper the tinker was resting with his dog by the fire, when the dog started to growl. On removing the brush-wood the tinker saw a huge monster with fiery eyes and long black body. His dog immediately rushed at it and engaged it in battle. A long fight ensued, until finally the monster dashed towards the loch and plunged into its depths with an unearthly snarl, the dog fastening on to it as he sprang. Long did the tinker wait, but his dog never returned. On certain calm days (so the story goes) the surface of the loch is said to be violently troubled, due to the continued fight between the monster and the dog, as they rise to the surface, each struggling incessantly to loose the other's grip.

When we pass from fiction to facts, as authenticated by contemporary newspaper reports, it is hard to discredit the existence of a strange creature in the waters of Loch Ness.

One eye-witness who saw it one February afternoon in 1932 described it as being from six to eight feet long (other observers have said thirty to forty feet) with a broad humped back, a swan-like neck and a small head with a jaw filled with rounded teeth. This observer described the monster as " paddling " slowly up against the current, which was running very swiftly, as the river Ness was in heavy spate at the time.

One man viewed the monster as it was crossing the main road between Dores and Foyers. He narrated that it had a long neck, which first came into sight as it crossed the highway, followed by a bulky body; but he could see no tail. The creature appeared to be carrying a lamb or small deer on its back, and moved with a jerky motion.

Another person declared he was taken aback by seeing a huge beast " for all the world like a camel," as he left Dores Inn, appearing through the foliage on the east side of the main road, as it was growing dark. He said he saw it " waddle across the road " and down the bank in the direction of the loch, where he lost sight of it in the trees; but he distinctly heard a great splash coming from the direction of the water, shortly afterwards.

Other witnesses have described a serpentine head and neck protruding above the surface of the loch. On one occasion, the monster was observed for forty minutes through powerful field-glasses as it lay basking on the surface of the loch, and eight separate humps were counted on its back.

The late Sheriff Watt of Drumbuie, Drumnadrochit, emphatically stated he saw the monster on several occasions while fishing the loch.

The spoor of the four-toed amphibian, discovered on the southern shore of the loch and reproduced in *The Daily Mail* was believed to be that of the monster. With new evidence continually flooding in from sources that are unimpeachable, it becomes palpable that some beast of huge dimensions does actually inhabit Loch Ness.

The monster of Loch Oich

Although in recent years it has been somewhat overshadowed by its more famous neighbour in Loch Ness, the strange beast that inhabits the depths of Loch Oich is well known in Inverness-shire tradition.

Many natives and also visitors to the district claim to have seen this monster; and *The Northern Chronicle* of 13th August, 1936, contained an account of a close view obtained by three English tourists who were boating at the Laggan end of the loch when they saw emerging from the water a " weird-looking creature," black in colour with two humps like a camel, a snake-like neck and body, and a shaggy head like a dog's. The monster remained " on view " for a few seconds only. Other people have described it as being like a huge otter.

Loch Treig

A noted race of water-horses was for long believed to inhabit Loch Treig, in Argyllshire. They were said to be the fiercest of their breed in the world.

The Rev. Dr. Stewart wrote of them that if anyone were to suggest to a Lochaber or Rannoch Highlander that the cleverest horse-tamer of his acquaintance could " clap a saddle on one of the demon-steeds of Loch Treig, as he issues in the grey dawn, snorting " . . . he would answer, with a look of mingled horror and awe—" Impossible! the water-horse would tear him into a thousand pieces with his teeth and trample and pound him into pulp with his jet-black, iron-hard, unshod hoofs!"

It is interesting to recall that a diver (a Government official) who carried out experimental investigations within recent years in Loch Treig, vowed he would never dive again into the depths of that loch. He confessed that the appalling creatures which he beheld at the bottom of Loch Treig baffled wildest nightmares. He collapsed on reaching the surface and it is said that he suffered from nervous disorders for a considerable time afterwards as the result of what he had seen.

The monster of Loch-a-Choin

There is a chain of three beautiful lochans in West Perthshire —Loch Ard, Loch-a-Choin and Loch Arklet—situated by the main road between Aberfoyle and Inversnaid. It is with Loch-a-Choin (The Dog Loch) that this story deals. Tradition attributes to this loch a water-monster in the shape of a huge dog.

Not so very long ago, one oppressively hot summer's day, a weary tourist sat down by the banks of Loch-a-Choin to have lunch. Soon he heard the sound of the rattle of pots and pans mingled with footfalls on the road behind him; and on looking round observed on the highway a tinker, laden with various metal cooking utensils, trudging along the road in company with a young lad. To his astonishment, he saw the tinker suddenly seize the boy, and walking down to the edge of a ledge of rock, fling him into the water. Immediately after the splash of the body, there was a great swirl, and the savage head of a huge and grotesque dog-like monster broke the surface and with one mighty gulp swallowed the body of the child whole. The tinker thereafter mysteriously vanished from sight. Terrified beyond all measure, the traveller fled to Aberfoyle as fast as possible. On entering the Inn he met some of the local people and told them of his weird experience by the shores of Loch-a-Choin.

He was told that what he had just seen was the recurrence of a tragically true event which had taken place on the banks of the loch many years ago, at the same place where he had rested for lunch, and that the tinker had been found out and hanged for his evil deed. The hiker had seen the murder re-enacted on the exact date and at the exact hour when the crime was originally perpetrated.

To this day, many of the older inhabitants of the district believe that the dog-monster still lurks within Loch-a-Choin, waiting for victims.

Morag of Loch Morar

The deepest freshwater loch in Great Britain, Loch Morar, also possesses its monster, named " Morag." According to the late Mr. Alexander Macdonnell, of Meoble:—" Some years ago, we were proceeding one morning down the loch in the estate motor launch from Meoble to Morar pier with some school-children and other persons on board. As we were passing Bracarina Point, on the north side, some of the children excitedly shouted out: " Oh look! What is that big thing on the bank over there? " The beast would be about the size of a full-grown Indian elephant, and it plunged off the rocks into the water with a terrific splash." Loch Morar's monster is said to have been seen by a number of persons of unquestionable veracity—" a huge, shapeless, dark mass rising out of the water like a small island."

Loch na Mna

The " wild beast " of Loch na Mna (The Woman's Loch) in Raasay is now no more. Tradition has it that this creature for years terrorised the neighbourhood by carrying off women and children to its lair until it was lured ashore by a blacksmith (afterwards called Alastair na Beiste—Alexander of the Monster) who killed and roasted a sow in his hut near the loch. A favourable wind blew the savoury smell over the water. Then, according to Boswell in the account of Dr. Johnson's Hebridean Tour, " the monster came and the man with a red-hot spit destroyed it."

The monster of Strathhalladale

Many years ago, a girl in a Caithness parish incurred the wrath of a local " wise woman," who pronounced on her a terrible " guidhe " (curse).

Like Titania in " A Midsummer Night's Dream," she was put under a " geas " (spell) to love a monster. The girl laughed at the old woman, and soon forgot the curse.

When she grew to womanhood, she married a man from Strathmore, and on their wedding day he was bringing her from Strathhalladale to his home when they were overtaken on the moor by a dense mist. They lost their way, and came upon a lonely bothy in which they took shelter for the night. They contrived to light a fire, and were sitting by it when without announcement or salutation a strange being entered the bothy—in form like a handsome young man; but goat-bearded, goat-faced and with the tail of a horse.

" Who is to have this woman? " asked the monster. " Who," said the man, " but he to whom she belongs." To this the satyr replied, " Let us fight for her." Then they began to fight, and under the man's hard blows the monster was soon lying on the ground.

Then an amazing thing happened. His wife, hitherto so gentle, rushed to the help of the monster, and turned on her husband with the fury of a demon. Horror-struck at her disloyalty, and unable to strike a woman, he realised that his only alternative was flight, and made for home with a heavy heart.

After a few days his wife appeared at Strathmore, apparently cured of her infatuation; but in due course she had a son who resembled the monster, especially in the possession of a tail.

This story, with a different setting, is given as authentic by the late Dr. Alexander McBain in a paper delivered to the Gaelic Society of Inverness in 1888. Descendants of the son, each distinguished by the possession of a tail, are said to be still alive, " not a hundred miles from Bonar Bridge."

Cnoc na Cnoimh

Nearly eight hundred years ago, a terrible scourge fell upon the fertile valley of the Cassley, in Sutherland. A fierce monster had taken up its abode in a hole on the east side of a hill in the vicinity, and no living thing was safe from its fury. In shape, the monster was like a huge worm, and if it had ventured out into the open, people might have learned how to avoid it, for worms are not as a rule noted for their speed of movement. But this monster's power lay in its venomous breath, which poisoned all that came within reach of its rapacious jaws. As a rule the worm lay hidden in its hole, breathing out noxious vapour like the smoke from a volcano. So powerful was its breath, that it hung over the countryside for miles, bringing certain destruction to all living things. The valley soon became desolate, and the people of the district fled from their houses.

At intervals, the worm left its lair and crawled slowly to the summit of the hill, winding its sinuous length round and round; and on these occasions, it used to lie as if surveying the scene of desolation round about with the greatest satisfaction. The hole in which the monster lived came to be called " Toll na Cnoimh " (Worm's Hole), and the hill round which it coiled itself " Cnoc na Cnoimh " (Worm's Hill).

William the Lion, King of Scotland, heard of the misfortune which had befallen this part of his realm, and offered a large reward to anyone who would slay the monster. But none of his knights was brave enough to attempt such a perilous task, and when no one came to their rescue the country folk lost heart, for it seemed as though they would have to go on living in fear all their lives. At last a rough-and-ready farmer from the Kyle of Sutherland—Hector Gunn by name—came forward and said that although he was a plain man he would try to slay the beast and rid the countryside of it for good and all. He mounted his horse and rode till he came to within a few miles of " Cnoc na Cnoimh." He asked the people where the Worm's Hole was ; but they answered that the monster was not in the hole that day, but had crawled up the side of the hill and lay sunning itself on the top as if like " an Diabhull " (the Evil One) he thought that all the world was his.

The farmer then wheeled his horse round and rode straight for the hill. He had with him a broadsword with which to sever the creature's head; but he soon found that this would not avail him at all, for before he came near to the foot of the hill, he felt the worm's poisonous breath coming towards him in waves of fetid heat, and became so weak and faint that he could go no further. He returned crestfallen to where the people were waiting for him, and great were their lamentations on seeing his dejected mien, for he had gone out full of confidence that he would deliver them from the scourge. " It is a good thing that the worm was asleep," they said, " or else Hector Gunn would have been utterly consumed."

Hector Gunn did not intend to allow himself to be beaten by a worm, not even by one with such unearthly powers as this. When he had recovered somewhat from his faintness, he borrowed a seven-ell-long spear, and asked the astonished villagers if they had any pitch. They said that they had, and he ordered them to boil some of it in a pot. He then went on to the moor and cut a great divot of peat. He thrust the end of the long spear through the peat, and dipped it in the boiling pitch. With this strange weapon in his hand, he mounted his horse once more and rode towards " Cnoc na Cnoimh." The country people followed at a distance, wondering. As soon as Hector Gunn came near the monster and it opened its mouth to suck him in with its poisonous breath, he held out the spear with the reeking peat at the end, and the wind blew the fumes right into the worm's face. So strange and pungent was the smoke that the creature was almost suffocated, and drew its breath, and wound itself tighter and tighter round the hill in its agony.

Hector rode nearer and nearer, till he was on a level with the monster, then with one quick movement he thrust the burning peat down its throat and held it there until the fearsome creature died.

Thus was the valley of Cassley delivered from the worm; and William the Lion rewarded Hector Gunn with gifts of land and money. And—to this day, men may go to " Cnoc na Cnoimh" and see traces of this old story in the spiral indentations said to have been made on the hillside by the worm as its coils tightened in its death throes.

The wild beast of Barriesdale

In the parish of Knoydart there is a loch which because of its dark, deep and gloomy waters is called Loch Hourn (Gaelic for " Hell "). This loch was for long believed to be haunted by " The Wild Beast of Barriesdale." It was said to have only three legs—two fore and one behind. Nothing could divert it from its direct route. It jumped over fences and even crofts; neither river nor loch could stop its course.

In the year 1880, this monster was encountered by a crofter who lived on the shores of the loch. He described it as a huge, three-legged beast with gigantic wings, which he saw flying towards him across the hills of Knoydart. Up to the time of his death, this man used to relate how he was pursued by the creature as far as his cottage, where he just succeeded in slamming the door in its face.

The creature of Loch Voshmaid

Told by George Ross, Corriemulzie, Sutherland

During the time of the following incident I was head stalker to the late Sir Samuel Scott. One day, a friend of mine (a guest of Sir Samuel) went to Loch Voshmaid in North Harris—known in the district as " The Enchanted Lochan." He took with him a new fly which he stated possessed supernormal powers. He had no luck that day, but had a great story to tell round the dinner table that night.

" As my new fly failed to move a fish," he said, " I resolved to try the worm from off a steep bank at a corner of the loch. For a long time nothing happened. Then all of a sudden, I got a terrific tug and my rod bent nearly double! As I proceeded to haul in my line, the head of a huge and grotesque creature appeared in front of me and its tail lashed out on the surface about a quarter of a mile away, near the bank on the opposite side of the loch. This monster ran out every foot of line from my reel, and just as I was being drawn into the water after my rod, I heard the sound of fairy bagpipes. A door opened in the hillside opposite and a troop of ' Wee Folk ' trailed the whole fish, tail first, into a hole in the rocks. Then my line snapped, the door closed and my fish was gone! I could still hear the pipes playing underneath the ground as I packed up."

The monster of Vayne

In the parish of Fern (Gaelic, " fearn "—an alder tree) in Forfarshire, stands the Castle of Vayne, on the edge of a glen on the north bank of the Noran River.

Only the gable wall on the east still stands, for part of the castle was blown up by gunpowder, and the stones since used for building dykes. The only roofed part of the building now remaining is a vault on the ground floor of the east wing, under which is believed to be a deep dungeon, into which the Lindsay family are said to have thrown all their treasures before taking their final departure from the Castle.

Several people have searched for the entrance to the dungeon with its treasure trove, but only one person is believed ever to have found it. According to the legend, he was just about to descend when he was forcibly thrust back from the aperture by a monster in the shape of a horned ox, which then departed in a blaze of fire through a hole in the wall—still pointed out!

Before the terrified man could recover his senses, the opening closed once more and the treasure was hidden from view for ever.

The black dog of Soluschraggy

On the burn of Kilphedder in Sutherland is " Soluschraggy " (Rock of Light) on which the sun shines during the short time it is visible in winter. This provided for the people of the " Taobh-dorcha "—the opposite and dark side of the strath— the only sign that it had risen at all, hence the name.

Below Soluschraggy, where the farmhouse of Dalial once stood, is a small lochan, scarcely more than a pool of stagnant water. There is a story that in a vault under the water is a hoard of gold guarded by a monster like a big black dog with two heads. It is said that a tenant once had the loch drained, and all the water carried off; but the poor farmer did not reap any reward from his labours. The monster came to visit him and made the hills echo with its terrible howling. For days this unearthly serenading went on, always at the midnight hour, until the man in desperation filled up the drain, and the waters of the lochan once more covered the treasure.

An archer and a monster

Malcolm Canmore is said to have had a monstrous animal like a crocodile which he kept on a small island on the Dee, near Braemar, known to some of the old people as " Eilean na Tadd " (Island of the Monster), and now called " Eilean na Meann " (Island of the Young Roe). The inhabitants of Braemar were taxed for its support and had to give in turn a cow or other animal to satisfy its voracious appetite.

When it came to the turn of a woman named MacLeod, she felt the imposition to be very hard indeed. She had only one cow. Her son, a famous archer, managed to dispatch the beast with his arrows and was sentenced to death by Malcolm Canmore for his temerity; but was later reprieved—in a manner reminiscent of the story of William Tell.

The King had ordered the gibbet to be erected on Craig Choinnich (Kenneth's Craig); and the sentence was about to be carried out, when MacLeod's wife, with his young child in her arms, came to plead with Malcolm to spare her husband's life. This he refused to do; but ordered instead that the woman and child should stand on the opposite side of the river, at Tom-ghaineamh, with the width of the river separating them from the condemned man. A barley bannock was placed on the child's head to serve as a target; and MacLeod was ordered to let fly at it with one arrow. If he succeeded in hitting the target without injuring his wife or child, his life was to be spared; otherwise the sentence was to be carried out. The archer's aim was true, and the arrow struck the mark.

The King, faithful to his promise, extended his pardon to MacLeod and gave him a place in his body-guard. From his fearless action when under sentence of death, MacLeod received the additional appellation of " Hardy," and his descendants are known to this day as the " MacHardies " (i.e. sons of Hardy).

Loch Pityoulish

This loch, situated between the River Spey and the foothills of the Cairngorms, has an eerie reputation. It is said to harbour a water-horse, which, in defiance of the " each uisge " tradition, is black in colour. This animal is believed to inhabit a sunken " crannog " or prehistoric lake-dwelling, the site of which at the bottom of the loch may be seen on calm days deep down through the clear water.

According to local tradition, the black horse appeared one day many years ago to the young heir to the Barony of Kincardine as he played with other children by the side of the loch— as a coal-black steed decked out with a silver saddle, silver bridle and silver reins. The boys grasped the reins and mounted the horse, which galloped off with them to the loch, and only the young heir lived to tell of the encounter, as he alone had had the presence of mind to free his fingers from the reins with a knife.

Bran and the monster of Achanalt

Strath Bran, between Achanalt and Achnasheen in Wester Ross, together with the river of the same name, and Loch Bran, about a mile to the west of Achanalt Station, is said to derive its name from Bran, the famous dog of the Feans, who disappeared for ever from the world of men somewhere in the strath.

The Ossianic legend runs that the Feans were hunting in Carn na Béiste (Cairn of the Monster), a round, high hill on Achanalty Moor, opposite Aultdearg. In the cairn there dwelt a ferocious monster, after which the hill had been named, as well as a small loch—Loch na Béiste—to the south of the hill. The hunters saw the beast in the distance, and Fionn sent his dog Bran to attack it.

Bran is one of those strange hounds of Celtic legend, described by Ossian as snow-white, with blood-red ears. No dog was fiercer than Bran in combat with man or beast; but when he came near the monster and beheld its hideous aspect, his courage failed him and he fled back to his master with his tail between his legs. A second time Fionn urged him to attack, but once more Bran slunk back through the heather and crouched down behind his master in a state of abject misery.

Amazed and angry at this display of cowardice, Fionn is said to have spurned him with his foot. Bran ran down the hillside till he reached the level strath, and there near the river bank, he burrowed a hole in the ground and quickly disappeared from sight.

When Fionn and his companions arrived at the hole, he was beyond reach, and would not come out in spite of all their entreaties. The Feans then decided to dig him out, but the deeper they dug the deeper Bran entrenched himself.

At last water rose in the hole, and they were forced to stop digging. The hole filled with water, and the loch formed is known as Loch Bran to this day.

Fionn, we are told, wept for Bran.

The monster, according to local tradition, still inhabits the cairn and the adjacent loch; but no one since the days of the Feans has ventured to intrude on it.

The kelpie of Corryvreckan

Many years ago, Beltane Eve rejoicings were going on at Moy, not far from Loch Buie, in Mull. When the bonfires were blazing, and the dancing and revelry were at a height, there appeared a young and handsome stranger, mounted on a white steed, who seized the loveliest of the village maidens, swung her into the saddle before him, and galloped with her over mountain and moor and rock to the dark sea-shore.

He then dismounted, and asked the maiden if she would be his " a so suas a chaoidh " (for evermore). Bewildered by this tempestuous wooing, and weary after travelling the rocky roads on horseback, the girl asked if he was taking her to some dwelling across the sea, or if he had a ship waiting for her, as she fain would rest. To this he replied:—

"I have no dwelling beyond the sea,
 I have no good ship waiting for thee.
 Thou shalt sleep with me on a couch of foam
 And the depths of the ocean shall be thy home."

Only then did she realise that she had been carried off by none other than the dreaded " Kelpie of Corryvreckan," who could assume man's form at will. She turned her eyes on the horse, and saw that its saddle was of seaweed, its bridle of pearl, and its bit of coral. Its mane was like the froth of the waves; and as she gazed, it plunged into the billows and became one with the foam of the sea. Its erstwhile rider then seized her in his arms and bore her with him into the green depths. The maiden's shrieks were heard above the loud roaring of the blast, as they sank

"Down to the rocks where the serpents creep
 Twice five hundred fathoms deep."

Next morning, a fisherman saw her corpse floating near the shore, and recognised her by her lily-white skin and golden hair. She was buried under a rock on the shore, with the dirge of the waves for her requiem. Every year on Beltane Eve it is said that the Kelpie gallops across the green on his sea-horse swift as the wind, with the mournful ghost of the maiden held fast on the saddle before him.

The monster of Loch Garten

Amid the Abernethy Forest in Strath Spey lies lovely Loch Garten darkened by pine woods and birch trees.

Tradition has it that a large carnivorous water-monster—a cross between a huge bull and a large stallion—used to haunt the neighbourhood where a burn (about $\frac{1}{4}$ mile long) flows out of Loch Garten into Loch Mallachie, through thick woods. This ugly creature, believed to prey on children and lambs, was described as having a jet-black mane, big head, broad back and glistening eyes. It wandered forth at night-time and its roars were to be heard echoing amongst the hills.

According to a local story, an old crofter from Nethy Bridge, decided to capture the beast, and one afternoon hitched the end of a long rope round a large boulder weighing several tons, on the shore of Loch Garten, at the other end of which he affixed a gaff-hook which he baited with a lamb. After he had coiled the rest of the line into a dinghy, he pushed off from the bank and paid out the rope yard by yard as he rowed towards the centre of the loch. When he had come to the end of the cordage, he heaved the baited hook (which he had appropriately weighted) overboard and rowed back to land as the afternoon was drawing to a close.

All through that night, there was a tremendous storm. Over and above the roar of the thunder and the noise of the tempest, came the fiendish snarls of the infuriated monster.

In the morning, after the storm had subsided, when the old man returned to the loch-side, not a trace of the huge rock could he discover. All that could be seen was a long deep-rooted rut along the trend of the sand leading down to the water's edge where the boulder had been dragged into the inky depths by the monster, which has not been seen or heard of since.

Dragons

While there is hardly a loch or corrie in the Highlands that has not its reputed " Big Beast," Celtic tradition has few stories of " beithrichean " (dragons). The dictionary definition of a dragon is " an imaginary animal, something like a winged crocodile," and story-tellers through the ages have added to and improved on this description until we get a picture like the following (given by L. H. Dawson in his " Stories from the Faerie Queen "):—

" Its body was loathsome, and vast as a mountain; it was sheathed with scales and when it roused itself the noise was like to the clashing of a thousand mail-clad knights. Its wings filled in the air like sails larger than were ever seen on ship, and its outrageous tail, armed with two lethal spikes, swept the plain for three furlongs round. It had most terrible claws, but a far more harrowing sight than any of these was its hideous head, with its grimly gaping maw displaying three ranks of iron teeth that dropped blood. Clouds of smothering sulphurous smoke poured from its throat and nostrils, and through the smoke its eyes blazed like beacons; and thus it advanced, bellowing loud defiance."

The legends concerning " The Dragon of Strathmartine " in Forfarshire; " The Ben Vair Dragons " (Beithrichean Beinn Bheithir) of Glencoe and " The Beast of the Charred Forests " (Peat Fire Flame) are all fairly well known.

Loch Scavan

Loch Scaven, with its two beautiful wooded islets, lies in Glencarron, Ross-shire, under the towering mass of Meruisg.

It is said to take its name from the Gaelic word " Sgamhan " (lungs or " lights ")—all that was supposed to remain of a person devoured by a water-horse. Many stories are told in the neighbourhood of an " each uisge " which had its dwelling in the loch, and which frequently appeared as a sleek, well-fed horse grazing by the roadside. When an unwary traveller approached the beast remained quietly until it was caught and mounted, then it immediately rushed into the loch with its victim, for whom there was no possible escape. Afterwards, the liver floated ashore—the only evidence of the disaster.

This seems to have happened very frequently in the Strath-carron district; at any rate the loch is known as Loch Scaven to this day.

The Ben Vair Dragons

Ben Vair, at whose base tourists to Glencoe are landed, got its name from a dragon which long ago took shelter in a great hollow in the face of the mountain, right above what is now Ballachulish Pier—known as " Corrie Lia." From the edge of the corrie, this dragon (tradition says it was female!) overlooked the path round the foot of the mountain, and would leap down and tear to pieces any unsuspecting traveller who attempted to pass.

No one dared to attack the dragon, and no one could think of a plan for her destruction, until Tearlach Sgiobair (Charles the Skipper) came to Ben Vair. He anchored his boat some distance out from the site of the present pier, and built a bridge of empty barrels between the vessel and the shore. The casks were lashed together with ropes, and bristled with iron spikes. When the bridge was made, he lit a fire on board the boat and placed pieces of meat on the embers.

When the odour of burning flesh reached Corrie Lia, the dragon jumped down in a series of mighty leaps to the shore and from there tried to make her way out over the barrels to the boat. The spikes, however, pierced her scaly hide, and tore her flesh so badly that she was nearly dead before she reached the other end of the bridge.

Charles the Skipper had meanwhile rowed his boat further out, so that a gap was left between it and the last barrel of the bridge. The dragon had not sufficient strength left to leap to the deck of the boat, nor to return the way she had come; so she died of her wounds where she was, at the end of the bridge.

The people of Ben Vair now felt at peace; but a new danger soon threatened. The old dragon had left behind her in Corrie Lia a whelp which in time became full-grown, and gave birth to a brood of young dragons which she hid in a corn-stack at the foot of the mountain! When the farmer discovered them in his stack, he at once set fire to it, hoping to destroy the brood. The shrieking of the young dragons was borne on the wind up to Corrie Lia, and the mother leapt down to their assistance. In spite of her efforts, however, they were burned to death; and when she saw this she lay down in her grief on a flat rock near the shore, and lashed the rock with her tail until she killed herself.

The rock upon which Ben Vair House now stands, is still known as Leac-na-Beithreach (The Dragon Rock).

Water-kelpies

An old pamphlet, dated 1823, refers to water-kelpies as follows:—" In the former and darker ages of the world, when people had not half the wit and sagacity they now possess, and when, consequently, they were much more easily duped by such designing agents, the "Ech Uisque,"or water-horse, as the kelpie is commonly called, was a well-known character in those countries. The kelpie was an infernal agent, retained in the service and pay of Satan, who granted him a commission to execute such services as appeared profitable to his interest. He was an amphibious character, and generally took up his residence in lochs and pools, bordering on public roads and other situations most convenient for his professional calling.

His commission consisted in the destruction of human beings, without affording them time to prepare for their immortal interests, and thus endeavour to send their souls to his master, while he, the kelpie, enjoyed the body. However, he had no authority to touch a human being of his own free accord, unless the latter was the aggressor. In order, therefore, to delude public travellers and others to their destruction, it was the common practice of the kelpie to assume the most fascinating form, and assimilate himself to that likeness, which he supposed most congenial to the inclinations of his intended victim.

The likeness of a fine riding steed was his favourite disguise. Decked out in the most splendid riding accoutrements, the perfidious kelpie would place himself in the weary traveller's way, and graze by the road-side with all the seeming innocence and simplicity in the world. . . . But this horse knew better what he was about; he was as calm and peaceable as a lamb, until his victim was once fairly mounted on his back; with a fiend-like yell he would then announce his triumph, and plunging headlong with his woe-struck rider into an adjacent pool, enjoy him for his repast."

Loch A'Garbh Bhaid Beag

This story is told by John Falconer, Achlyness, Sutherland

One afternoon in the autumn of 1938, Mary Falconer, a woman of Achlyness in West Sutherland, was taking a short cut with a companion through the hills to Ardchullin with some venison in a sack slung over her shoulder.

On nearing Loch Garget Beag, she noticed a number of ponies grazing by the loch-side. Thinking that one of the beasts—a white one—was her next-door-neighbour's sheltie, and that she would make use of it for carrying her heavy load on its back the rest of the journey to Rhiconich, she walked towards the animal.

As she came within a few feet of it, however, she discovered that it was a much larger pony than her neighbour's, and to her astonishment, she saw round its neck, entangled with its mane, a cluster of water weeds.

The eyes of the animal and the woman met; and in that instant she sensed that she was looking on an " each uisge " and on no ordinary beast.

To her amazement, there and then the whole group of about thirteen ponies, on noticing her, galloped to the edge of the water, and plunging into the loch, sank below the surface in front of her eyes.

Her companion corroborated her story in every particular.

The people of Kinlochbervie and district are firmly convinced that Loch Garbet Beag houses in its depths not one water-horse, but a whole herd.

(Mary Falconer is well known locally as a " Seer." There is hardly a funeral in the district that she does not forecast. Not only does she " see " funerals before they take place; but counts the number of conveyances and recognises the mourners. On one occasion, she saw the long grass and bracken sway beneath the pall-bearers' feet as they carried the coffin—long before the actual death occurred.)

The Monster of Loch Canisp

According to Mr. Kenneth Mackenzie, of Stoer, Clachtoll, Sutherland: " While rowing a load of peats across Loch Canisp (Loch Feith an Leothaid) in Assynt, and when about three-quarter way over, a huge creature suddenly reared up four five feet over the stern of my boat. It had a long neck and a head which resembled that of a hind, only it had no ears. The beast stared at me for roughly a quarter of a minute, before disappearing below the surface in a terrifying swirl. It was autumn, and it was growing dark at the time: It was a horrible experience: I got such a fright, that I never rowed faster for the bank in all my life."

Shortly afterwards, Neil Mackinnon, keeper on the Assynt Estate, had a similar experience one evening on the same loch. He described the monster in similar terms, adding —" I was pertrified with fear when I saw a long neck with a flat earless head rise out of the water close to my boat. The grotesque animal had eyes like saucers: When I regained by senses, I made a bee line for the shore. I don't think I ever rowed harder before. It was just growing dark, and I ran all the way home."

Both are men of high integrity and not given to exaggeration.

The Strathardle water bulls

Unlike the " each-uisge " the " tarbh-uisge " (water bull) was quite harmless, and did not interfere with those who came near its haunts.

It lived in small lonely tarns among the hills, from which it emerged only at night. Its lowing was heard after sundown— a weird sound " like the crowing of a cock "—as it came from its lair to graze with the farmer's cattle; but it was seldom seen.

Calves born with short ears, or, as called in the Gaelic, " corc-chluasach " (knife-eared) were said to be the offspring of the " tarbh-uisge." It had no ears itself, and hence its calves had only half ears!

An eye-witness account of the water bull, from Lorne, describes it as a small black animal, velvety and soft in appearance.

A water bull is said to have been slain with a bow and arrow at a lochan high up on the Mullach Sgur of St. Kilda; and the marks of cloven hoofs found on the grassy slopes round Stallar House on Breray (one of the St. Kilda group) were attributed to the " tarbh-uisge."

The lochs of Lundavra and Achtriachtan, in Glencoe, were long famous for their water bulls; and a belief in existence of the " tarbh-uisge " persisted until very recently among the dwellers beside Loch Rannoch and Loch Awe, where many farmers were in the habit of carrying guns loaded with silver coins (usually sixpences), to be discharged when the beast appeared—silver alone having any effect on such animals.

A water-bull was long believed to inhabit Cultalonie Pool, on the River Ardle, near Kirkmichael, Perthshire. It was often seen grazing with the domestic cattle, and was recognised by its jet-black coat and entire absence of ears.

This " tarbh-uisge " seems to have been of gentle disposition, until attacked on one occasion with a gaff (or landing-net) by a fisherman who mistook its black, silent presence beside him as he cast his line in the river.

Its peaceful nature changed into a lust to kill, and it was believed to lurk thereafter among the reeds and boulders by the waterside, seeking whom it might devour. It became known as " The Demon Bull of Cultalonie." It left behind it an enormous " corc-chluasach " (knife-eared) progeny; and descendants of these bulls were pointed out in the district by the older inhabitants until recently. These bulls had evidently inherited their fierceness from their " tarbh-uisge " ancestor, and were very wild.

Many years ago I recorded an amusing local poem (which I gleaned from a Kirkmichael worthy) about a particularly fierce descendant of the Cultalonie " tarbh-uisge " known as the " Dounie Bull ":—

" Whaur's the road to Coltie Pool?
    Follow doun the dyke;
Gin ye're soople, loup the ditch,
    That should be na fyke.

Past Aldchlappie through the haugh
    Step ye canny by;
That's whaur Tinker Mary's man
    Strangled puir Mackay.

Follow the Ardle by the field
    Whaur they've sown the rye;
But mind and watch the muckle bull
    As ye pass the kye.

Gin that Dounie bull gaes wude,
　　Faith!　It's fashious wark;
Dinna get his dander up
　　Crossin' through the park.

Ance he tossed Chick Stewart's dug,
　　Gied him sic a clure;
Then he charged a fisherman,
　　An' made him rin like stour.

Weel, I've warned ye; but some folk
　　Winna tak' advice.
What?　Ye'll gang anither way?
　　Gad!　I think ye're wyse!"

Loch Derculich, in the Vale of Tay, was believed to house a most formidable " tarbh-uisge " which, less than 130 years ago was frequently observed sauntering along its shores. At peat-cutting times especially it was often seen; but no one ever examined it, as all took to their heels whenever they saw it.

5

MERFOLK

" A thousand phantasies
   Begin to throng into my memory,
   Of coiling shapes, and beckoning shadows dire,
   And airy tongues, that syllable men's names
   On sands, and shores, and desert wildernesses."

Merfolk

Bodach Capan Dhearg

The " Merfolk " were the traditional inhabitants of the sea. There are few accounts of mermen; but Highland and Island lore teems with allusions to the mermaids who dwelt—

" Fathoms deep beneath the wave,
   Stringing beads of glistening pearl "

and who often came up from the sea-caves to disport themselves on the shore, and were to be seen in the quiet bays, floating on the surface of the water and mingling their voices with the sighing breeze.

To this day, belief in merfolk, the traditional inhabitants of the briny deep, is rife, especially in the north-west coastal districts of Sutherland.

Mermen are known by their red caps which they wear (hence the term—" Bodach Capan Dhearg ") when they disport themselves amid the breakers, while mermaids on the other hand, are said, on occasion, to come up from the sea-caves to recline on the shore in quiet bays and are recognised by their reddish-yellow curly hair with wreaths of sea-weed round their necks and shoulders. They are believed to mingle their voices with the sighing breeze, but these mermen are said to fight savagely if entangled in fish-nets, and unless instantly released cast death-spells upon the neighbourhood.

During August, 1949, mermen were sighted off Craig More in the Parish of Kinlochbervie by several crofters and sailors on more than one occasion.

In the superstitious belief of the North, seals held a far higher place than any other of the lower animals. They were believed to have a mysterious connection with the human race, and to have the power of assuming human form and faculties.

Seals occasionally lift themselves perpendicularly out of the water exposing half their bodies and look as like the representation of a mermaid as possible. The wild and mournful cry of the seal is difficult to describe—something between the mew of a cat and the howl of a dog in distress—a weird and unpleasant sound which harmonises with the wild scenery of their surroundings. Highlanders are by no means prepossessed in favour of the good looks of a seal or " sealgh " as they term it. " You are a sealgh " is an expression of disgust which, when uttered by one crofter to another, is considered a great insult and a climax to every known term of reproach.

In Caithness, seals were said to be " fallen angels "; and a popular saying in the north is that they are " clann righ fo gheasaibh " (king's children under enchantments). Their origin is explained as follows:—

The widowed King of Lochlinn married for a second time a lady skilled in the Black Art, who by its means strove to get rid of her step-children. It took her seven years and seven days to perfect a plan; and at the end of that time she put the royal children under a powerful " geas " (spell) by which they were transformed into seals—neither fish nor flesh. When at sea they would yearn for the land and when on land would long for the sea " as long as the waves beat upon the shore." They were allowed to resume their original human form three times a year at full moon.

There is a sect in North Uist known as " Clann is Codrum nan ròn' " (the MacCodrums of the seals) who are said to be the descendants of the " enchanted " seals.

It was considered for a long time to be most unlucky and nothing short of murder, to kill a seal, and many tales are told of the fate that befell any brave enough to perform the dire deed. Misfortune was said to dog the footsteps of such a man till the day he died—like the punishment of Coleridge's Ancient Mariner who shot the sacred albatross.

The mermaid's grave

Included by the courtesy of Sir Arthur Waugh, past-President of The Folk-Lore Society.

" My story of an encounter with a mermaid at close quarters comes from the little island of Benbecula in the Hebrides.

Somewhere about 1830, the islanders were cutting seaweed or " kelp," a fertilizer, on the shore when one of the women went to wash her feet at the lower end of a reef. The sea was calm, and a splash made the woman look up, and out to sea. What she saw caused her to cry out, and the rest of the party, hurrying to her, were astonished at the sight of a creature ' in the form of a woman in miniature,' some few feet away in the sea.

The little sea-maiden, unperturbed by her audience, played happily, turning somersaults and otherwise disporting herself. Several men waded out into the water and tried to capture her, but she swam easily beyond their grasp. Then a wretched little boy threw stones at her, one of which struck her on the back.

She was next heard of a few days later, but, alas, then she was dead; her body was washed ashore, about two miles from where she was first seen. A detailed examination followed, and we learn that ' the upper part of the creature was about the size of a well-fed child of three or four years of age, with an abnormally developed breast. The hair was long, dark and glossy, while the skin was white, soft, and tender. The lower part of the body was like a salmon, but without scales.'

The lifeless body of the little mermaid attracted crowds to the beach where she lay, and the Highland spectators were convinced that they had gazed upon a mermaid at last.

But the story does not end here. Mr. Duncan Shaw, Factor (Land Agent) for Clanranald, baron-bailie and sheriff of the district, after seeing the corpse, gave orders that a coffin and shroud be made for the mermaid, and, in the presence of many people, she was buried a little distance above the shore where she was found. The Factor was unlikely to be credulous, and that he ordered a coffin and shroud for the strange little creature cast upon his shores suggests that he thought she was at least partly human."

ALEXANDER CARMICHAEL, *Carmina Gadelica*.

Actually, the alleged mermaid was interred in the presence of a large assemblage of the Hebridean people in the burial-ground at Nunton, where her grave is pointed out to this day. I have seen it myself. R. M. R.

The mermaid of Mackay

A story told by W. J. Mackay, F.S.A. Scot., Skerray, Sutherland

In the middle of the eighteenth century there lived on the banks of a river in the Mackay country a man known as " Big Hector." His great delight was to wander along the shores of the bay near his homestead, where this stream flowed into the sea. Among the flotsam and jetsam cast on the beach he could be found, and especially during dark winter nights when the wind would be howling through the high cliffs, which sent a pang of fear through the hearts of the bravest inhabitants. The stronger the elements of Nature, the greater did the desire appeal to Hector to wade among the surf in the house of darkness. Such was his love for this kind of life that he was shunned by many and left alone to his desires; but this did not seem to affect him. He attended to his solitary cow, cooked his own meals, and did not interfere with anybody. When he did speak, his talk was always of the sea, and the strange creatures which dwelt there; but few believed his tales.

In this mode of life he continued to live for well over thirty years, until one morning, following one of the greatest storms known within living memory, he surprised his neighbours by his extraordinary activity around his croft. He seemed much happier and more industrious than usual and it was observed that he seemed to have left off his former habits. He, however, evaded any enquiry into his affairs, and it was no small wonder when within a year of this strange change in his manner, the cries of a young child were heard from the open door of his cottage. Despite such happenings, the inside of his house was outwith the gaze of his neighbours. He would not encourage them in any way, nor would he satisfy their curiosity in regard to the cries they heard issuing from within. So it was no small wonder when it was whispered from mouth to mouth that Hector had been taken command of by the " Wee Folk." His way of life just desired that and what could be expected—what more could he expect? The ways of a child, however, are the same in all ages and in all places, the wonder of what lies outside their home sets them exploring. A passing neighbour, herding his cow along the banks of the river, happened to lift up his head and on seeing the child, he, like one possessed, left everything and ran towards the village, shouting as he went that Hector had a child.

As years rolled on, Hector seldom went along the shores of the bay. The villagers occasionally visited him and became friendly with his mermaid wife and child, Peter. Peter joined in the life and laughter of the other children of the community, as he was now about five years old. It was, however, noticeable that Hector would not allow anyone near the thatch of his cottage.

One morning, Hector and his young son went for fuel to the moor. As they rounded the turn of the hill, the mermaid mother came to the door of her home, and her sobs and yearning cries after her son were heard by most of the villagers.

An hour or two later, Hector was on his return journey with his son running by his side, when suddenly, letting out a piercing cry, he threw down his creel of peats, and hastened towards his croft.

A wall of foam could be clearly seen moving towards the open sea, and the music of the seals floated over the water.

Hector went straight to the thatched roof of his house, took one look, and then rushed inside his cottage. No one was there, and his hidden treasure was gone. The veil of his wife had disappeared. As long as he could hide this from her, she was his; but now she had managed to get possession of it, and had gone back to her ocean castle.

Hector dashed along the banks of the river; but the procession heading seaward increased their speed, and all he could hear was the music and splashing of the waters.

Broken-hearted and dismayed he returned to his lonely croft. His son tried to console him, but could not do so.

The following morning, he again went to the river's brink, and there he found a large salmon on its bank. This followed morning after morning. One night he kept watch, and sure enough the old seal came up the river with a salmon in its mouth which it laid on the water's edge.

Peter grew up to be a fine young man and married. No one knew so much about the sea and its ways as he did, likewise the generations which followed him.

The mermaid of Cromarty Firth

" Of all the old mythologic existences of Scotland," writes Hugh Miller in his " Scenes and Legends," " there was none with whom the people of Cromarty were better acquainted than with the mermaid."

The mermaid of Cromarty Firth was often seen on moonlight nights, sitting on a rock near the shore a little to the east of the town of Cromarty, singing and braiding up her long golden hair.

Many years ago, a Cromarty shipmaster, John Reid, fell in love with the village heiress—Helen Stuart. She, however, spurned his advances and as weeks passed into months, the unhappy man's grief grew greater instead of less. He began to take long solitary walks by the edge of the bay, communing with

himself and trying to think of some plan to win the affections
of the girl.

One evening as he walked on the shore as the sun was setting,
he heard the low notes of a song, coming from a rock opposite
the famous Dropping Cave. On turning the corner of the cliff,
he saw the singer—a beautiful girl—sitting half on the rock
and half in the water. Her fair hair rippled over her snowy
shoulders, and the rays of the setting sun were reflected with
dazzling brightness from her forked tail which moved gently in
the water. She was looking towards the cave as she sang, and
her song was re-echoed from its mouth.

Reid realised that he was looking on the mermaid; but to
one as much in love as he, her bright beauty meant nothing. He
had heard of her alleged power over the destinies of men, and
to him this encounter meant a chance to invoke supernatural
aid to gain the hand of Helen Stuart. With grim determination,
he crept towards her over the rocks and grasped her in a grip
of steel. The last note of her song lengthened into a shriek
and an expression of terror came over her lovely features. Like
a snake, she coiled and writhed to free herself; but Reid held
on, till at last her struggles grew fainter and she lay passive on
the rock.

She spoke; and her voice was as clear and cool as the sea.
" Man, what do you want with me? " she asked. Still unmoved
by her beauty and pathos, Reid in a gruff tone replied, in the
prescribed formula—" Wishes three." His first wish was that
neither he nor any of his friends should perish by the sea; his
second—that he should succeed in all his undertakings; and his
third—that Helen Stuart should become his bride. " Quit and
have," the mermaid answered. The man slackened his hold,
and " pressing her tail against the rock until it curled to her
waist, and raising her hands, the palms pressed together, she
sprang into the sea. The spray dashed to the sun; the white
shoulders and silvery tail gleamed for a moment through the
green depths of the water."

Reid lost no time in seeking out Helen and relating a highly-
coloured account of how he had mastered single-handed, one
of the most dreaded monsters of the ocean—A mermaid! He
omitted, we may be sure, any mention of his three wishes. His

motto appears to have been " All's fair in love and war "; and the story does not show him in a very good light. Helen, however, seems to have been easily gulled; Hugh Miller relates how when returning home after hearing his story she " leaned for support and protection " on his arm; and that she became his bride soon afterwards.

The merman at Port Gordon

In 1814 a merman was sighted off Port Gordon in Banffshire. He was seen by two fishermen returning from the fishing one afternoon. About a quarter of a mile from the shore, they observed quite close to their boat a creature with its back towards them and half its body above the water. In appearance it was like a man sitting with his body half bent. In colour it was tawny yellow. The noise made by their boat as they approached to get a closer view made the creature turn round. They saw he had a swarthy face, short greenish-grey curly hair, small eyes, a flat nose and a large mouth. His arms were exceptionally long; and below the water they could see that his body tapered into a fish-tail.

The merman gazed at them fixedly for a moment or two, then dived from sight, to reappear some distance away along with what the fishermen took to be a mermaid. Alarmed at what they had seen, they made for the shore with all speed.

Caithness mermaids

Many mermaids have been reported and vouched for in the far north-east of Scotland.

A Miss Mackay wrote an account of her own experience in 1809 while walking with a friend along the desolate coast of Caithness. She saw what looked like a human face above the water, but decided that it could not belong to a human being, as the sea was too wild and wintry for anyone to be bathing; and besides, the object disappeared for long periods at a time under the water. Miss Mackay could not on the other hand agree with her practical-minded friend's suggestion that they were looking on the body of some drowned animal, tossed to and fro by the waves; for every now and then a slender white hand rose above the water and tossed back a long mane of green hair!

The lady was convinced that she had seen a mermaid; and when her report was published, James Munro, schoolmaster at Reay, wrote a letter to a London newspaper describing how, twelve years before, he had seen what he took to be a mermaid in Sandside Bay. He had been walking " an gob na tuinne " (at the water's edge) when he saw sitting on a rock jutting out into the sea a female figure " in the action of combing its hair, which flowed about its shoulders, and was of a light brown colour."

" It remained on the rock," Mr. Munro wrote, " three or four minutes after I had observed it, and then dropped into the sea, from whence it did not reappear to me. I had a distant view of the features." He concluded his letter with the words:—

" I can only say of a truth that it was only by seeing the phenomenon that I was perfectly convinced of its existence."

The mermaid of Kessock

A legend from the Black Isle

A man named Paterson was once walking along the shore near Kessock Ferry, when he saw, " 'na suidhe air an aigein dhorcha " (sitting on the dark misty deep), a mermaid, whom he tried to detain by wading into the water and pulling some of the scales from her tail, in obedience to the old belief that if even part of her fish-tail was removed, a mermaid was compelled t assume human form. Before his eyes the transformation took place, and the sea-maiden stood up before him, tall and fair. She had long, silky hair that was as yellow as gold and soft as the curling foam of the sea; her eyes were wide and clear and blue as the sky; her lips were as red as winter berries and as tempting as fruits of summer—and in place of the fish-tail she had slim white feet.

Paterson fell desperately in love with the sea-maiden and took her home as his bride. The scales he carefully hid in an outhouse.

He lived in a cottage by the shore; and " nuallan nan tonn " (the raging noise of the waves), which sounded night and day at the foot of tne cottage garden, filled his mermaid bride with longing to return to her home in the land-under-the-waves where she had been " nursed by the ocean and rocked by the storms." She used to plead with her husband to let her go, promising that if he did so their family would always be blessed with a plentiful supply of fish, and that no members of it would ever be drowned at Kessock Ferry; but he remained adamant.

One day one of the children, named Kenneth, discovered the scales in the outhouse and took them to his mother, who straightway made for the shore and became a mermaid again.

Not since that day has the mermaid of Kessock been seen; but there are still local people who firmly believe in her existence, and declare that she still watches over her descendants and keeps them from peril at sea.

The mermaid on Duncansby

A Caithness fisherman, walking on the shore one morning, saw a beautiful girl sitting on a rock, singing as she combed the long yellow hair which fell over her lovely shoulders. He saw that she had a tail like a fish, and knew that he was looking on a " maighdean mhara " (mermaid). Approaching quietly, he clasped her round the waist. She looked up at him; and in that moment came the realisation that each was meant for the other.

From that time the young man kept daily tryst with the maid of the sea who brought him gorgeous jewels, gold, and silver, which she said she found among the wrecks of ships in the Pentland Firth. Neighbours began to wonder about the source of his sudden wealth which, alas, soon went to his head. He demanded more and more treasures, which he gave in presents to girls of the district; and while dallying with them often forgot to keep his tryst with the mermaid, who grew jealous, and upbraided him for his unfaithfulness.

One day she was waiting for him in a boat, in which she offered to take him to a cavern near Duncansby Head, where she kept guard over all the treasure ever lost in the Firth. Overjoyed by the prospect of such wealth, he jumped into the boat, and they sailed away to the wonderful cave.

When they reached it, he fell asleep to the sound of her singing; and when he awoke he found himself secured by golden chains in the innermost recesses of the cave, surrounded by lumps of gold and bars of silver.

> " Bags of fiery opals, sapphires, amethysts,
> Jacinths, harxtopaz, grass-green amethysts,
> Beauteous rubies, sparkling diamonds."
>
> MARLOWE.

There, according to the legend, he has been confined ever since; and whoever finds the cave (and overcomes the mermaid) will have jewels worth a king's ransom.

An Inverbervie mermaid

Many years ago, a Forfar landowner nearly lost his life by rushing into the sea at Inverbervie after a mermaid. He was standing on the shore when he heard a commotion in the water, and saw a woman's head above the breakers, her white arms waving. Thinking that she was someone out of her depth, he prepared to swim to her assistance. As he entered the water, her struggles increased, and she called to him in a despairing voice. The would-be rescuer was swimming towards her with powerful strokes when he felt a stone whizzing past his head, thrown by his man-servant on the shore. The missile struck the water near the wailing figure, who without a sound sank below the waves. The man swam back to shore and demanded an explanation of his servant's strange action. " That wailing woman," he was told, " is not a human being but a mermaid. If you had touched her, she would have dragged you down and drowned you."

As he spoke, they heard the sound of mocking laughter coming towards them, and the mermaid was seen swimming away in the dusk.

The mermaid and the bagpipes

Many years ago, there lived near Gairloch, West Ross-shire, a man who was very anxious to learn to play on the bagpipes: but after much effort, he had made little progress. One day he walked down to the shore and saw a mermaid. He knew that if he could catch her she would grant him whatever he wished, so he got hold of her and asked his wish. " Is it to please others you want to play or to please yourself? " she said. " To please myself, of course," he said. Then she gave him his wish, and he played and played on the bagpipes ever afterwards. His playing pleased himself immensely; alas, it pleased nobody else!

Mermaids in Orkney

In the year 1890, a mermaid was seen at Deerness in Orkney. She reappeared two years later, when she was sighted by some lobstermen working their creels. They described her as small, with a white body and long slender arms, and black hair. Sometime afterwards, a creature believed to be this mermaid was shot not far from the shore, but the body was not recovered. In June, 1893, another mermaid was seen by the people of Deerness " a' sigheadh " (disporting herself) in the summer sea.

About the same time, a farmer's wife at Birsay was gathering seaweed when she saw a strange creature lying in one of the rock-pools. She went back for her husband, and the two returned in time to get a good view of the unusual figure. Their descriptions coincided; the woman speaking of the mermaid as " a good-looking person," and her husband describing her as brown. (In this connection, it is interesting to note that whereas in all the traditional mermaid stories the maid-of-the-sea has golden hair, in eye-witness accounts it ranges in colour from green to black!)

The farmer and his wife tried to capture the mermaid, but, as J. M. Mackinlay writes in his " Folklore of Scottish Lochs and Springs "—" in the interests of folklore, if not of science, she managed to escape! "

The mermaid was quickly lost to sight beneath the waves; and her appearance has not again been reported.

The three wishes

Mermaids were believed to have the power to grant " wishes three " to any mortals quick enough to steal up and catch them unawares.

A Ross-shire seaman once came upon a " maighdean mhara " sitting on a rock near Whiteness Point at Tain. He crept up to her unheard and unseen, and seized her in his arms. The mermaid begged him to let her go, but the seaman, who was very strong, held on to her, and said that he would not loosen his hold till she had granted him three wishes. On being asked what they were, he replied, " Health, wealth and happiness." " Your wishes are granted," said the mermaid, who then plunged into the sea and vanished from sight.

A similar story is told of a crofter in Skye, who found a mermaid asleep on a rock in the sunshine, and released her only when she had granted his three wishes—that he should have the power of foretelling the future; that he should be able to cure the King's Evil (scrofula), and that he should acquire skill in music.

Another tale, narrated by J. H. Dixon in his " Gairloch: Its Records and Traditions," published in 1886, is still believed in in the district where the incident is said to have occurred:—

A certain Ruraidh (Roderick) Mackenzie, the " elderly and much respected boatbuilder at Port Henderson," went one day when a young man to a rocky point of the shore, where he saw a mermaid sitting on a rock facing the sea. He seized her by the hair, and she cried out in great distress that if he would let her go, she would grant him whatever boon he might ask. It was not recorded whether or not Mackenzie knew that he was entitled to three wishes: at any rate he made only one request— that no one should ever be drowned from any boat that he might build. The mermaid pledged her word that this would be so, and he released her. Throughout Mackenzie's long business career, his boats continued to defy the winds and waves; and Mr. Dixon somewhat naively adds: " I am the happy possessor of an admirable example of Rory's craft." *Quod erat demonstrandum* !

The mermaid and the Lord of Colonsay

Many years ago, there lived on the island of Colonsay a young chieftain renowned for his prowess in battle. He was betrothed to a beautiful lady whom he loved dearly, and their wedding-day had been fixed, when a message came across the sea from the King of Scotland asking the Lord of Colonsay to help him to drive off a horde of fierce invaders threatening to take his kingdom.

The chieftain ordered his ship to be made ready, and went to bid farewell to his lady. She gave him a ruby ring, telling him to wear it always for her sake. " As long as my heart is yours," she said, " the jewel will glow with blood-red fire." He then set off for the wars.

On reaching the mainland, he fought with the King against his enemies, and overcame them. Once more he set sail for his native isle.

The sea was calm and the rowers strong, and when daylight had faded and the moon was casting its silvery gleams over the water, the boat was within sight of the island.

Full of joy at the prospect of meeting his lady so soon, the young chieftain could not sleep; but paced the deck, looking out across the waves to the land ahead.

Suddenly he saw, reclining on the crest of a wave, a most beautiful maiden, with golden hair reaching to her waist, and great blue eyes. Thinking that she must have fallen overboard from some other ship, he called to the crew to cease rowing. But they either would not, or could not obey him; and the boat sped swiftly on. Then the Lord of Colonsay remembered all he had heard of the merfolk who dwelt in the caves of the ocean, and a shudder crept over him at the thought that he was looking on one of their number. His affection was fixed on the lady he had left on Colonsay, and he had no desire to be tempted by a mermaid's siren wiles. He drew back, but as the boat swept past, the sea-maiden stretched out a white hand and seizing the unfortunate man round the waist, dived down with him into the depths of the sea.

The boatmen, who had seen nothing of this, soon missed their master, and came to the conclusion that he had fallen overboard; and carried back this sad news to the people of Colonsay. They mourned him as dead, but his lady held to the belief that he would one day return alive and well.

Meanwhile, the young chieftain had been carried down through the ocean by his captor. Green and purple distances were above him, and green and purple distances below. He saw the sea-monsters heaving past, and the hulks of wrecked ships, and the bones of drowned mariners; and further down, where gloom gave way to gloom, vast livid tangles of seaweed that coiled and writhed like living things. At last she brought him to a wonderful region at the bottom of the sea, where the floor was yellow sand and the roof was the dark blue ocean. Here there were hundreds of caves, all opening out of each other, and the sand was covered with pink coral, and mother-of-pearl; and there were jewels, and cups and plates of gold and silver half-buried in it, that had been taken from the holds of wrecked treasure-ships.

Here the sea-maiden tried by all her wiles to persuade the chieftain to stay, leaning over him so that he could feel the softness of her yellow hair, and could gaze into the depths of her blue eyes. She spoke to him, and her voice was low and honey-sweet. But he spurned all her advances, and springing to his feet, demanded to be taken back at once to the land above the sea.

" Think better of it," cried the mermaid. " If you will not stay with me willingly, I shall place you in a cave, the entrance to which is barred by the sea, and there you shall remain for ever, and your lady will waste her life waiting for your return. Think better of it, and give me your love."

" Never," replied the young chieftain, declaring that he would rather die than be false.

As he spoke, the pink coral and the yellow sand, and the treasure-trove vanished from sight; and he saw in front of him only a black, gaping hole, across which the waves dashed, barring any exit. The mermaid plunged through the hole into the sea, lashing the water to fury with her tail.

The chieftain was left alone to mourn his fate and to sigh for his island home and for his lady. He often looked at the ruby ring on his finger and saw that it still glowed brightly, and he knew by that that his lady had remained faithful to him. The sight of the blood-red stone always gave him renewed courage.

One day the mermaid swam into the cave, looking more beautiful than ever, with a jewelled comb holding back her golden hair. She spoke gently to him, and promised to let him go if he would grant her one favour.

When he asked her what she wanted, she replied, " your ruby ring." She had of course no intention of letting him go if he gave it to her, but knew that once she had it in her possession, she could find a way to send it to the lady as a proof of her lover's death. Then, she reasoned, the lady would wed someone else, and the knight, believing that she had been unfaithful, would lose all interest in her, and would be content to dwell for ever under the sea.

But the chieftain saw a chance of escape if he promised to grant her request. He said that he would gladly give her the ring if she would do him a favour in return. " Carry me once more to the surface of the sea," he said, " and let me look for the last time on my beloved island. Then I will give you the ring."

She bore him upwards through the water to where the stars

looked down on Colonsay, then held out her hand for the ring. The chieftain slipped from her grasp and gave a mighty spring on to a ledge of smooth rock that ran out from the shore.

Mad with rage and disappointment at having been outwitted by a mortal, the mermaid dived from sight beneath the waves. The people of Colonsay believe to this day that when they sail over the spot where she disappeared, they can hear the wild lament which she sighs for ever under the sea for the chieftain whom she loved and lost.

A John o' Groats seal legend

Some years ago, there lived near John o' Groats house, in a small cottage by the shore, a man who made his living by catching seals and selling their skins.

He laughed at the idea that it was unlucky to kill seals and said that they were most worth killing of all animals, for their skins were so large that he got a good deal of money for them.

One day a dark stranger, mounted on a gigantic horse, rode up to his croft. He called to the seal-catcher to come out, saying that his master desired to do business with him. The seal-catcher was delighted, and climbed up behind the dark horseman. He soon began to gasp for breath, so fast did they go.

" The cold winter's wind that was before them, they overtook her; and the cold winter's wind that was behind them, she did not overtake them. And stop nor stay of that full race did they make none, until they came to the brink of the sea." There on the edge of a precipice the horseman pulled up his steed and said, " We have almost reached my master's dwelling." As he spoke he went to the edge of the cliff and looked down. The seal-catcher did the same, and saw nothing but the lonely sea and the grey sky. " Where is your master? " he asked. For answer, the stranger clasped him in his arms, and leapt with him over the precipice. As they passed through the cool darkness of the ocean depths, the seal-catcher found that he could breathe quite easily. He felt neither pain nor discomfort; but only an increasing sense of wonder.

At last they came to the bottom of the sea. There were hundreds of seals, young and old, stretched out on the sandy floor of the ocean, and on looking round, the seal-catcher saw that his guide had turned into a seal also. He led him to where an old grey seal lay, moaning with pain. Nearby lay a blood-stained knife, which he recognised as his own. Then he remembered that some hours before he had stabbed a seal which had plunged into the sea with the knife in its back.

" That is my master," said his guide, pointing to the wounded seal. " It was your hand that wounded him, and your hand alone can heal him."

Bitterly ashamed of what he had done, the seal-catcher bound up the wound to the best of his ability, and the old seal rose up strong and well again. The guide said that he would take the seal-catcher home, if he would promise never again to hunt seals. This he promised gladly.

The guide changed into the shape of a man once more, and taking the seal-catcher by the hand, rose with him through the waves. The horse was waiting on the top of the cliff, and they mounted it once more and galloped like the wind till they reached the seal-catcher's cottage.

The seal-catcher dismounted, and the stranger handed him a bag of gold, then reminding him of his promise, wheeled his horse round and passed swiftly out of sight.

The seal-catcher kept his word, and never again hunted seals. He prospered and lived happily ever after.

The Breckness man and the seal

Near Breckness there are some rocks much frequented by seals, and one Christmas morning a Breckness man saw a " selchie " asleep on one of the rocks. Creeping up to it, he shot it dead with his gun. He took the carcase home, skinned it, and boiled part of it for oil.

Shortly afterwards, his only cow died from some unknown cause, and the man attributed its death to his shooting of the seal.

Next Christmas morning the same man was walking near the shore when he saw another " selchie " lying in the same position asleep. This time, however, he did not shoot; but went home immediately lest he would be tempted to kill this one also and so bring more misfortune on himself, so great was his belief that the death of his cow had been a judgment on him for the shooting of the seal.

A Shetland seal story

A Shetlander was once on his way to the fishing, early in the morning, when he came upon a large seal lying asleep on a rock. He approached it cautiously and stabbed it with his knife. The wounded animal floundered off the rock and swam away with the knife still embedded in its flesh.

Some time afterwards, the Shetlander went with others to Norway to buy timber for building in their treeless island.

In the first house they entered, he saw in one of the rafters, the knife with which he had tried to kill the seal. Overcome with fear, he sought to leave the house; but the Norwegian householder took down the knife from the beam and returned it to its owner, warning him never again to disturb an innocent seal taking a rest.

The grey selchie of Sule Skerrie

The rocky islet of " Sule Skerry " (skerry of the solan goose) some twenty-five miles west of Hoy Head in Orkney, is to this day the resort of thousands of seals—or " selchies " as they are called in Orkney. There is a very old Orcadian ballad with the above title which tells of a maiden who dwelt in Norway who fell in love with and married a seal-man called " Hein Mailer." Shortly after their marriage he disappeared, and the maiden was left to weep as she rocked her infant son on her knee.

One day as she sat by the shore, a " good grey selchie " came and sat down by her feet. The seal addressed her in human speech and said:—

> " I am a man upon the land,
>   I am a selchie in the sea;
> And when I'm far frae every strand,
>   My dwelling is in Sule Skerrie."

On hearing this, the girl realised that she was looking on none other than her husband, transformed once more into a grey seal. The " selchie " disappeared as suddenly as it had come. At the end of seven years he returned—this time as a man—and put a gold chain round the neck of his son, who thereafter followed him on his journeyings.

With the passage of the years, the woman forgot her seal-husband and married " a gunner good " who went out one May morning and shot two—an old grey seal and a younger one. Round the neck of the younger animal he found a gold chain; and when he brought it to his wife, she realised that her son had perished, and gave vent to her grief:—

> " Alas! alas " this woeful fate!
> This weary fate that's been laid for me!
> And once or twice she sobbed and sighed,
>   And her tender heart did break in three."

Sea-trows and finmen

Others of the " Daoine-Mara " (folk of the sea) were the Orcadian " sea-trows " and the " Finmen."

The sea-trows were believed to dwell in the sea-washed caverns. They were described as " great rolling creatures " that tumbled about in the water, alarming the fishermen. Whenever they appeared, they were instantly beaten off with oars and staves. From descriptions given of them, the sea-trows may well have been " porpoises."

The " Finmen " were believed to be somewhat like Eskimos in appearance, and were credited with driving away the fish.

In 1681, one was reported as having been seen sailing up and down in a little boat off the south end of the Island of Eday: and another was seen three years later off Westray. The dearth of fish which followed these appearances was attributed to the Finmen.

Night lights

Occasionally at night a strange and unaccountable light is seen out at sea off the west coast of Sutherland. The local people call it " Teine " (fire). This light, or fire, has been observed travelling at considerable speed, and is believed to foretell calamity or disaster. Seen from the Kinlochbervie shore it is termed " The Assynt Light " (" Teine Assynt ") and viewed from the Assynt coast it is known as " The MacKay's Light " (" Solus MhicAoidh "). The cause of this peculiar phenomenon still remains a mystery; but at times, this midnight fire which sweeps the Minch is very bright.

On winter nights, when there is peace on sea and land, the " Fir-chlisneach " (Nimble Men, or Merry Dancers) come forth to dance in the northern sky. Such is the poetic explanation given by the romantically-minded Celt of the scientific phenomenon known as the " Aurora Borealis," those

> " Fearful lights that never beacon
> Save when Kings or heroes die."

Another name for the Northern Lights is " The Streamers," and it is said that when they have a battle among themselves, as often happens, the blood of the wounded falls to the earth and becomes congealed in the form of "blood-stones," called in the Hebrides " fuil siochaire " (elf's blood).

Eilean-nan-Sithean

There are many parts of the Scottish Highlands where mysteries are still unsolved. In certain districts of Wester Ross a belief in the supernatural still prevails. " It is the land of the edge of moorlands and the ruins of forests and the twilight before dawn, and strange knowledge dwells in it." The depths and remoteness of the solitude, the huge peaks, the deep chasms between the rocks, the dark gloom of the primeval forests, the deep black lochs—are full of associations of awe and grandeur and mystery.

In the dark waters of Loch Torridon, there is a tiny weather-beaten rocky islet of not more than two acres, adorned with fir trees and grasses. It is locally known as Eilean-nan-Sithean (Fairy Island).

No one has set foot on its shores for years. The Fairy Isle does not like to be visited, and the inhabitants of Shieldaig, the nearest hamlet, avoid the place. They do not use its rich grass for grazing their cattle and sheep, for it is said to be haunted by an evil spirit. At night-time, when the wind moans in the corries, they whisper, round the peat fire, the legend of a fisherman who wooed a mermaid and later deserted her. She in turn, lured his frail boat to the treacherous rocks of Eilean-nan-Sithean, and dragged him to his doom in the loch.

Ever since that day, no living creature has lived for more than a few hours on it, and no birds ever rest or nest there.

The Blue Men of the Minch

The " Blue Men " have been seen only in the Minch, and chiefly in the strait which separates Lewis from the " Shiant Isles " (charmed islands). The Sound is called after them " Sruth nam Fear Gorm " (Sound of the Blue Men). They are said to be of human size and of great strength. Night and day they swim round and round and between the Shiant Isles, and that is why the sea there is never at rest. They have been described as blue-coloured, with long grey faces that they raise with their long restless arms above the waves.

" Sruth nam Fear Gorm " has often been called " The Current of Destruction " because so many ships have been swamped there. Sailors were afraid of the Blue Men, who were said to take a mad delight in attacking ships; and many sailed round the Shiant Isles instead of taking the short cut between them and the Island of Lewis.

A ship is once said to have come upon a blue-coloured man asleep on the waters. He was taken aboard and bound hand and foot till it was impossible for him to get away. The ship had not gone far when two Blue Men bobbed up above the water and shouted:—

> " Duncan will be one, Donald will be two;
>
> Will you need another ere you reach the shore? "

On hearing this, the captive snapped the ropes that bound him as if they had been made of straw, and leapt out of the boat into the sea.

There is a boatman's song about the Blue Men, the last verse of which runs:—

> " Oh, weary on the Blue Men, their anger and their wiles!
>
> The whole day long, the whole night long, they're splashing round the isles;
>
> They'll follow every fisher—ah! they'll haunt the fisher's dream—
>
> Where billows toss, oh, who would cross the Blue Men's stream? "

According to West Sutherland fishermen, the Blue Men are said to enjoy following steamers and other water craft on their way to and from Stornoway. They swim in groups or gangs and rise up above their waists in the water to attract attention. They are of a glossy-blue appearance and are distinguished from the mermaids on account of their bearded faces. They use their teeth as well as their arms and legs in battle. Some say that their appearance generally foretells stormy weather.

6

THE HIGHLAND VISION

The Highland vision

As the outward events of the world today grow more spectacular, the minds of many of us turn towards problems which do not lie easily on the surface. We begin to ponder upon ultimate issues and have recourse to those powers hidden behind the veil of appearances. There is no real security in the material welfare of today. Have our hopes that " Science " would spell freedom and joy been achieved? Anxiety fills the hearts of men and women in all walks of life. They begin to ask what really is happening to human life on earth.

So far as the Scottish Highlands are concerned, there is no chapter more extraordinary, and few more interesting, than that which deals with Second Sight. Much that is merely traditional has without doubt accumulated round the subject; but there still remains a considerable number of well-authenticated anecdotes that deserve the attention of both the investigator and the psychologist. Second Sight is a Celtic gift thought to be the remains of the magic practised by the Druids, and Second Sight has flourished more among the Highland people than any other race.

The familiar remarks: " I feel it in my bones," or: " I felt I just had to do such a thing," mean that the speaker has some sort of foresight or pre-warning about something about to eventuate. Well, this is just a form of Second Sight. Water divining (or dousing) is said to be the result of a reflex action caused by some stimulus in the mind beneath the level of conscious perception. If one accepts the fact of water-divining, it must follow as a matter of course that one admits extra-sensory perception in the form of " Second Sight " which is just a form of physical radiation, and this faculty still exists in the Highlands today.

To the Celtic temperament, there is nothing impossible in the theory of Second Sight—that singular faculty of " seeing " the invisible, which Dr. Johnston defined in his " Journey to the Western Isles of Scotland " as: " An impression made either by the mind on the eye or by the eye on the mind, by which things distant are received and seen as if they were present.

Three Gaelic words have been used to describe the faculty. These are:—DA RADHARC, DA SHEALLADH and TAIBH SEARACHD. Of these perhaps DA SHEALLADH is the commonest, and certainly the most interesting in its derivation. It means literally " The Two Sights." The vision of the world of sense, which normally we all possess, is one sight; but that of the world of the spirit is open only to certain people, who are then said to have " The Two Sights," or what amounts to the same thing—a Second Sight.

By means of this faculty, they see shades of the departed revisiting the earth, and the etheric doubles or phantasms of the living. The " Seer " or medium often guards, warns and advises against impending tragedy or calamity—or prepares a person to brace himself up to face some unavoidable calamity.

Although Second Sight must not be confused with ghost seeing, most of the instances recorded are associated with presages of death or of some other calamity. The phenomena can take several forms, the Seer detecting supra-sensible things which are quite outwith the range of perception of most people; for a heavy curtain obscures the vision of man, so that, unable to register the spiritual, he is only conscious of things to be seen, heard, felt, tasted and smelt.

A light often heralded a death, and was known as a " dead-candle " or " corpse-candle." It would be observed moving about the house and along the road by which the corpse was to be carried to the churchyard. This light was generally pale bluish, wholly unlike any made by human agency.

The crowing of a cock at or about midnight was heard in fear and trembling. This was regarded as the death-warning of a member or relative of the family. The roost would then be immediately inspected to ascertain in what direction the bird was looking, and whether its comb, wattles and feet were cold. If they felt cold to the touch, the death of one of the household or of one nearly related, was not far distant. " The ' crowing ' of a hen was regarded with special dread, and as the sure indication of death in the dwelling."

A dog howling at night portended death, and the Death Angel was to seize his victim in the direction towards which the animal was looking, and at no great distance. This superstition prevails among the Arabs, who fancy that the dog is then seeing Azrael, the Grim King. It was believed that a dog would not approach a sick person, if the sickness was unto death, and most minutely did the inmates of the house watch the conduct of the dog with any one that might fall ill.

If a white dove was observed approaching and hovering over a particular person in the early morning, this was reckoned a sure sign that that person would soon depart the earth

The apparition of the person would be seen wrapped in a winding-sheet and the higher the winding-sheet reached up towards the head, the nearer would be the death.

When one showed more than ordinary joy, it was regarded as an omen of death, either of himself or herself, or of one nearly related.

To dream of a white horse, was a sure sign of death.

To dream of a death was a sure sign of marriage.

If a sick person did not sneeze, the disease would end in death. Sneezing was accounting the turning-point towards recovery.

A more than usually good crop foreshadowed the death of a farmer, and was known as the " fey-crop."

If the body of the corpse was soft and flabby when the coffin lid was closed, it was a sure indication that another corpse would soon be carried from the same dwelling.

The chairs on which the coffin rested were overturned as soon as the coffin was lifted off them, and were allowed to lie, in some places until sunset, and in others till one of those that had attended the funeral returned, when they were lifted and carefully washed. If not overturned, the spirit returned from the unseen world.

A shower on the mould of the open grave meant that the soul of the departed was happy, but a hurricane disclosed some foul deed done, but never brought to light, or of a compact with Satan.

In the case of those who were supposed to possess in their lifetime other power than their own, a white dove and a crow have been seen to make a dash on the coffin in contest which should reach it first. Sometimes the dove gained the victory, and sometimes the crow—with such violence that it broke through the lid of the coffin. The dove was the emblem of the Spirit and the crow that of the Prince of Darkness.

The night after the funeral, bread and water were placed in the apartment in which the body lay. The dead was believed to return that night and partake of the meal. Unless this was done, the spirit could not rest in the unseen world. This curious custom seems to throw light upon what have been called " food vases," and " drinking-cups," found in round barrows and in the secondary interments in long barrows, supposed to be of the "bronze age" and of ancient British period. A burial ought not to be looked at from a window. The one that did so, would soon follow.

So soon as death occurred, all the doors and windows were thrown wide open, in order to give the departing spirit full and free egress, lest the evil spirits might intercept it in its heaven-ward flight. (The Eskimos have the same custom.)

Immediately after death, a piece of iron, such as a knitting needle or a nail was stuck into whatever meal, butter, cheese, flesh or whisky were in the house to prevent death from entering them. The corruption of these articles has followed closely on the neglect of this, and whisky has been known to have become as white as milk.

All the milk in the house was poured out on the ground. The chairs and other articles of furniture were sprinkled with water. The clothes of the dead were also sprinkled with water, and it was the common belief that they always had a peculiar smell. If there was a clock, it was stopped. If there was a mirror, it was covered, as were all the family portraits.

All the hens and cats were shut up during the whole time the body was unburied, from the belief that, if a cat or a hen leaped over it, the person who was the first to meet the cat or hen that did so, became blind, not perhaps at the time, but assuredly before leaving this earth. The neighbours did not yoke their horses, unless there was a running stream between the dwellings. No tillage was conducted during the time the corpse was lying unburied.

When the death took place, a messenger was despatched

for a wright, who hastened to the house of death with his
" strykin beuird." The body was washed, clothed in a home-
made linen shirt and stockings, " strykit " on the board and
covered with a home-made linen sheet. Many a bride laid up
in store her bridal dress, to be made into her winding sheet, and
her bridal linen and bridal stockings as well as her husband's,
to be put on when life's journey was ended.

When the eyelids did not close, or if they opened a little
after being closed, an old penny or halfpenny piece was laid
over the eyes. On the breast was placed a saucer or a plate
containing salt, to ward off evil spirits, because they dare not
come near Christ's savour of the earth, and a candle or two were
kept constantly burning beside the body, to prevent the Prince
of Darkness from coming near the body.

The coffin and grave-clothes were made with all-becoming
speed. When all was ready, a day and an hour were fixed for
the " kistan "—that is, for laying the body in the coffin, and a
few of the more intimate female friends and nearest relatives of
the deceased were invited to attend.

At the appointed hour they came, usually dressed in mourning. Then the qualities and deeds of the departed would form
the topic of conversation. To the other female acquaintances
that had not been present at the " kistan," invitations were sent
to come and take a last look at the dead.

The corpse was sedulously watched day and night, more
particularly, however, during the hours of darkness. The
watching during the night was called " the luke " or " the
waukan." A few of the neighbours would meet every evening
to act as watchers. One of them at least had to be awake lest the
evil spirits might come and put a mark on the body. The time
was ordinarily spent in reading the Scriptures, sometimes by
one and sometimes by another of the watchers, and all the
conversation was carried on in a subdued voice.

On occasions, the " waukan " was not so solemn. There
was usually a plentiful supply of new pipes and tobacco, obtained
specially for the purpose, and hence the irreverent sometimes
spoke of the " watch " as the " tobacco-nicht." Whisky was
also freely drunk, and in many cases tea or bread and cheese
with ale were served about midnight.

It was the prevailing idea that nothing would grow over the grave of a suicide, or on the spot on which a murder was committed. After the suicide's body was allowed to be buried within the churchyard, it was laid below the wall in such a position that one could not step over the grave. This was done under the belief that, if a pregnant woman stepped over such a grave, her child would quit this earth by its own act.

The instrument by which the unfortunate put an end to life was eagerly sought after, as the possession of it, particularly the knot of the rope, if death was brought about by hanging, secured great worldly prosperity. This notion about the knot of a rope by which one was hanged did not attach simply to a suicide's rope, but to a criminal's.

Still-born children and children who died without baptism were buried before sunrise, from the belief that, unless this were done, their spirits were not admitted into Heaven; but floated homeless through the regions of space. In some places they were buried in such a position that no one could step over their graves.

Funeral by night

Second Sight may be found in the Highlands today; but few local people care to admit it. In 1952, I received a letter from a crofter in north-west Sutherland, who confessed that he, with a friend, happened to be crossing the hill near Oldshore More at a late hour, when suddenly a funeral procession appeared. The night was remarkably fine with a full moon, which enabled them to see objects quite distinctly. They knew well that no interment would be taking place at that late hour Trembling with fear, both he and his companion managed to get out of the way of the cortege. He recognised himself among the mourners. The coffin was being carried shoulder high, as the procession passed them. After it had passed him, he turned round to have a look at it; but to his astonishment there was not a single trace of it. The procession had vanished. About a week later, he was one of the mourners in a funeral procession—travelling along the same route to the old churchyard by the seashore.

The wicked Lord of Melgund

On the verge of a steep bank of the Melgund Water in Forfarshire, stand the ruins of Melgund Castle, in the olden times the home of the head of the House of Lindsay, a family whose domains then extended from. Coupar-Angus to the Howe o' the Mearns.

One cold winter night a watchman was pacing alone round the ramparts. Every now and then he paused to listen for the approach of hostile forces. Suddenly he saw a hearse, drawn by four black horses with nodding plumes, slowly approaching the Castle. The hearse was followed by a great retinue of lords and knights, mounted on black steeds, and many hundreds of vassals and serfs on foot. As the funeral procession passed slowly on to the principal gate of the Castle, the warder saw to his terror that neither the hooves of the horses nor the feet of the mourners had left any impression in the snow.

As silently and slowly as it had approached, the sombre procession moved away from the Castle gate.

Above the howling of the wolves, the moaning of the wind, and the sullen roar of the river, the Castle bell began to toll, and the warder knew that someone had died within the Castle. Dawn was breaking with a soft, pale light in the east. His watch had ended, and he made his way down from the ramparts to the Chapel, where he found the priest kneeling before the altar, offering up prayers for the soul of the man who had died—Sir David Lindsay, lord of the castle and lands of Melgund. The warder told the priest of the vision that he had seen and the priest spoke to him of death-warnings sent from heaven, which only favoured mortals see.

Accustomed as he was in those days of bloodshed and violence, to hearing death-bed confessions of wicked deeds, the priest of Melgund Castle had that night listened to a tale so horrible that the memory of it was to remain with him until the day he died. Lord Lindsay had all his life mocked and spurned the Church; but that night when he felt his end was near, he had called for the priest to attend him. The priest spoke words of comfort, telling the dying man that all sins would be forgiven to the man who truly repented. Then Lord Lindsay beckoned to him to come nearer, and in a voice so low as to be almost inaudible, made his final confession.

" I was never married," he said, " to the lady known as my first wife. The marriage ceremony was a sham by which I cheated a woman who loved me with her whole heart. Shortly after her child was born, I poisoned them both. They were buried in the same grave; and I pretended to be distressed at their death. Shortly afterwards, I married again. For fifty years her spirit, with her child in her arms, has appeared nightly by my bedside in silent reproach more terrible than any verbal indictment of my crime."

He then fell back, never to speak again. The priest, sighing deeply, placed a crucifix on the breast of the dead man, and left the room.

Six days later, the body of Lord Lindsay was taken from Melgund Castle to be buried at Findhaven. The hearse, the coal-black horses with their nodding plumes, the mourners on horse-back and on foot—all corresponded in the smallest detail to the vision seen by the solitary watcher on the battlements on the night Lord Lindsay breathed his last.

" First " sight in the Highlands

One evening a Sutherland crofter was sitting outside his cottage door, when he saw a stranger coming along the road towards the house. He watched the man for some minutes till he took a branch path leading to the crofter's door. The crofter then stepped inside for a moment to inform his wife of the approach of a visitor. On going out again he was more than puzzled to find that the stranger had vanished. The house stands on a slight eminence with a good view of the neighbour-hood, but the astonished crofter could see nothing further of the stranger. None of the villagers whose houses he must have passed had observed him.

The crofter there and then gave a full description of the man to his wife and to a brother. In a short time the incident, uncanny though it was, was forgotten. Some months later a child of the same crofter was taken ill. The doctor, a young practitioner recently come into the district, was sent for, and in the course of the day the father was standing at the door of the cottage waiting impatiently for the doctor's arrival. At a bend of the road appeared the mysterious stranger of several months before. He was, of course, the expected doctor, but in features, dress, and appearance generally he was the exact counterpart of the individual who had formerly presented himself. On inquiry, it was ascertained that the doctor had never before been in the neighbourhood. The crofter, his wife and brother, most respect-able and estimable people, are still enjoying good health, and are fond of telling this strange story.

A Benbecula seer

I was staying with a friend at Creagorry, on the Island of Benbecula and was fishing a loch called Langivat. There is a church at one end of the loch, and my gillie said to me: " This is the loch where the minister's son was drowned some years ago. That is his father's church and manse." It appeared that the boy had been playing on the banks of the loch with friends, and had fallen into the water. The other children at once ran to the manse and told his father, who came with help. By that time the boy had disappeared and they were unable to find the body.

A member of the father's congregation was digging kelp on South Uist (the neighbouring island to Benbecula) when he suddenly stopped and thought: " The minister's son has been drowned in Loch Langivat and they cannot find him. I see the body and I will go over at once." He arrived at the loch with his long iron-handled pronged instrument for digging kelp.

He at once went and found the body of the minister's son and pulled it out.

I said to the gillie: " Is this true? It sounds ridiculous to me." He replied that the man was still alive. I was duly introduced to him, and asked him what it was that had made him go over to the loch. All he said was " I don't know why I went. I just had an impulse and felt compelled to go."

A Strath Oykell vision

One New Year's Eve, many years ago, a young shepherd in Corriemulzie, went to Oykell Bridge, Sutherland, the nearest hamlet—some eight miles distant—to call on some friends.

After paying his respects at Oykell Bridge, he called later on that evening at a crofter's house two miles up the Strath, where he spent some hours celebrating. The weather had been stormy and a previous fall of snow had slightly thawed and frozen. The main road was coated with ice to such an extent that it was practically impossible to walk along it, and people were forced on the verge of the adjoining hillside.

About ten o'clock the following morning, New Year's Day, a farmer went out to feed his cattle with his eldest son, a lad of ten or eleven. As they were passing the end of a cart-shed furthest away from the road, they noticed a figure, who they immediately recognised, walking rapidly down the hill. They both remarked on his sure grip on the ice.

The shepherd walked quickly and confidently down the icy road, and the farmer's little boy, rather curious, ran to the end of the building to see what fittings he had on his boots.

When the boy got there, the young shepherd had vanished. Later in the day, a message arrived from the shepherd's croft to say that he had not returned the previous night. A search party was sent out, and his footprints were followed in the snow where he had taken a short cut over the rocks on his way home. There the searchers found where he had slipped over a boulder and had been badly injured. He had crawled in the snow to where his dead body was found, and afterwards carried home.

A doctor was called, and gave the approximate time of death as between nine and ten o'clock that day—the time when the farmer and his son " saw " the figure walking down the hill.

"The Lights" on Loch Kinellan

A considerable time ago, a number of school children were spending their Christmas holidays at Strathpeffer. They went down one morning to call on an old woman who had a small croft. There had been a hard frost for the past week and the whole countryside was ice-bound.

The boys told the old woman of their intention to go sliding and skating on the frozen waters of Loch Kinellan on the following day. She raised her hands in protest, and in commanding tones, said: " Last night, I saw the lights on the loch, which from the time of my parents downwards, are a sure sign of disaster. On no account venture on to the ice, for each time I see the lights on the loch, they foretell a drowning in the parish."

The boys took the old woman's warning. The following night there was a rapid thaw. The ice gave way with a noise which echoed amongst the hills, and three local children, who had been sliding on the frozen loch, fell through and were drowned.

The Kilmorack disaster

Many years ago, I spent a holiday with friends who kept a well-known coaching establishment at Beauly. One night, a large black retriever dog howled piteously and perpetually throughout the night in a shed adjacent to the house. The dog was in the habit of sleeping in the shed perfectly peacefully.

I shall never forget the whines that the poor beast uttered, they were so strange and plaintive.

Old Mrs. M———, a native of the village, that night stated that she had a foreboding that some dreadful calamity was about to take place, and that the mournful whines of the dog were a sure foreshadowing of something evil. Nor was she wrong, for the following day a traction engine, on its way up Strath Glass, was pulling a tender up the dangerous incline, when at a bend on the road near Crask of Aigas, it plunged into the ravine of the Beauly River, a short way from Kilmorack Falls.

All aboard the engine and tender were killed outright. Their mutilated corpses were gathered together, and afterwards placed, for coffining, in the shed in which the dog had howled.

The widow of Strathspey

Many years ago, a man died in Strathspey, leaving a widow with a large family. This woman was said to possess " the two sights." Her husband had left very little money, and she found it necessary to pay great attention to the farm in order that her family might benefit. Among other things, she owned a mill, part of the grist of which she allowed to the miller, and took the rest to herself as rent in kind. She often walked down from the farmhouse to the mill to see if her share of the meal was regularly put in the allocated place.

One evening she remained longer than usual, and dusk was falling as she was returning to the house. Her path lay through a little wood, and she had to cross a burn over a temporary bridge made of fallen trees. The stream was in flood, and she was approaching it with some hesitation when she became aware of the figure of her deceased husband standing on the opposite side. He waded through the water towards her, took her hand, led her carefully over the bridge, and walked with her through the wood.

The phantom then chided her for rashly venturing out alone after dark.

When the woman reached home, she told her friends and neighbours, and showed them the faint mark on her wrist where the hand of her shadowy companion had rested. One and all were firmly convinced that what she had " seen " was the spirit of her dead husband, come to save her from threatened disaster.

John Henderson's aunt

Told by Mr. John Sutherland, Lybster

A Lybster merchant named John Henderson once walked to Wick on business one day. On his return journey in the dark, an old woman suddenly materialised by his side near Torran-reach, whom he at once recognised by her club foot, as his aunt, who lived at Lybster.

According to the story, neither spoke. Henderson thought she was following him for a joke. After following him for over a mile, his silent companion mysteriously vanished on approaching Occumster.

Henderson called on his aunt next day, and said, "That was a fine trick you played on me last night! "

" Trick? " said she, " the only trick I played on you was in my dreams when I pictured myself walking home with you, trying to keep pace with you, from Wick to Lybster, and felt very exhausted when I woke up in the morning! "

A death warning

A girl from Kinlochbervie, possessed with the gift of " The Sight " (" Second Sight "), was for some years house-keeper to a laird who lived in a lodge overlooking Badcall Bay, near Scourie, Sutherland. One afternoon in early spring, she saw her master drive away in his car. A short time afterwards, for no accountable reason, she began to feel very depressed, and sensed a sort of indescribable evil foreboding, which she tried hard to shake off, but could not. As she was cooking lunch, she was startled to hear footfalls in the house. Feeling very uneasy, for she was quite alone, she hurried into the hall, but found no one there, but she heard heavy footsteps ascending the upper portion of the stair. She distinctly heard her master's bedroom door open and a noise as if several persons were scuffling about in his room above. The room, however, was quite empty, and just the way her master had left it. Believing that she was imagining things, she returned to the kitchen.

All of a sudden a car drove up to the lodge. Answering a knock at the front door, she saw the local police officer, who informed her that he had received a telephone call to inform him that the laird had been drowned in a roadside lochan while attempting to rescue a lamb which had fallen into the water, and that he was on his way down in the police car to the scene of the accident. Having broken the tragic news, the police officer immediately departed. A short while afterwards, the laird's car arrived at the house with some people inside it and they carried the dead man up the stairs to his bedroom. The footsteps which she heard ascending the stairs with the corpse to the room above, corresponded exactly to the identical shuffling footfalls which she had heard about an hour previously. What actually had happened was that, seeing a lamb struggling in the water by the roadside, the laird threw off his kilt and plunged into the loch in an endeavour to rescue the animal; but the shock of the icy water proved too much for him and he died.

The Meikle Ferry tragedy

On a market day in Tain in the year 1809, several Sutherland crofters and Sheriff MacCulloch of Dornoch, crossed over in the ferry-boat. Towards evening, the shore on the Ross-shire side towards Meikle Ferry was crowded with those going home, and far too many climbed into the boat. It was a dead calm and the heavily laden vessel pushed off from land; but when it had nearly reached the middle of the ferry, and the deepest part of it, it lurched over on its side. The water rushed in, and all the occupants were thrown overboard.

About seventy people were drowned, and the sea gave up its dead one by one, until only the Sheriff's body remained below the water. A friend of MacCulloch's was deeply affected by his death, and had a dream in which the dead man appeared by his bedside, spoke of his sudden death, and described where his body lay. He added that the fish seemed to have been restrained from touching his body, which would be found unmutilated. The dream was fulfilled in every particular.

Sandy Campbell's funeral

One afternoon over half a century ago, Robert Inglis, who was at that time clerk to Forbes, the Factor to the Duke of Atholl, was walking down tht Great North Road in the direction of Blair Atholl with one of the former stalkers from Fealaar Lodge. This man, who was then residing with his sister at Stonfatriach, was employed that year as gillie for the shooting season.

Suddenly the gillie sprang to the side of the road and shouted out to Inglis: " Mind out, stand clear and let the funeral pass ! " but Inglis was amazed, as they were both quite alone together, and he could see no funeral whatsoever. However, the gillie insisted that a funeral procession was approaching them, going down the main road towards Blair Atholl, and after both men got to the side of the road, the ex-stalker started to name the individual mourners including Inglis himself, whom he described sheltering under " Cameron the Shop's umbrella! "

Inglis, who saw no funeral procession, treated the matter as a joke, or delusion, and enquired whose funeral it was; when immediately his companion informed him that it was Sandy Campbell's funeral—Sandy Campbell the Fiddler.

About six months afterwards, Sandy Campbell, who was all his life a strong and healthy man, died from blood-poisoning sustained while gralloching a stag.

The day of the funeral, Inglis received instructions from Factor Forbes to attend a meeting at Dunkeld. Inglis told Forbes that he would be back in time to be present at the funeral.

On leaving the train at Blair Atholl station, Inglis met a friend also on his way to the funeral service. They agreed they should walk slowly together along the road to meet the funeral party, and as they proceeded along the highway in a northerly direction, Inglis forgot the gillie's prophecy.

As they were about to cross over the Banavie Bridge, the funeral procession appeared in sight, and at that very moment the sky became overcast, a chill wind blew up the Glen, and a heavy mountain shower poured down. Stepping to the side of the road in order to let the cortege pass, Inglis's friend, Angus Cameron of the shop, Blair Atholl, suddenly put up his umbrella over their heads to protect them from the rain-storm.

The phantom card players

It was the custom in the old days that, when the Chief of a Clan went from home, his castle was guarded every night by some of his adherents, who took that duty by turns. This practice originated in the days when there was danger of a sudden attack by night; but in later and more peaceable times, it became a mere formality, and usually only one gentleman kept watch, bringing an attendant or two with him. The scene of the vigil was always the great hall of the castle.

One February night, a gentleman entered the hall of a castle in the North Highlands to keep vigil for his absent chief. He brought with him one servant—a mere youth—who had a considerable reputation as a " Seer." They were supposed to take it in turns to sleep, and the master, after watching till midnight, delegated his vigil to his servant.

The youth was interested in the novelty of the scene around him, and was examining some of the family pictures on the walls, when he was amazed to see the great folding doors suddenly thrown open, and two footmen in the family livery entered with lights. They were followed by members of the family who had been dead for years, and whose wan and ghastly visages had no resemblance to earthly inhabitants.

Card-tables were brought, and the ghostly company sat down to play. They conversed with each other as they played; but although the lad could see their lips moving, there was no sound of voices. He recognised in one of the footmen a relative of his own, who in his lifetime had served the Chief.

At dawn the shadowy troop returned the way they had come; and as they passed the youthful watcher, the man who had been his relative in life turned and beckoned to him.

At that moment his master wakened, and the poor visionary begged to be carried home, being quite unable by his own efforts to move from the spot where he stood. This was done, and the lad called his friends round him and related all that had happened, adding that the hand of death was upon him and that nothing could save him.

He died three days afterwards.

The child of doom

The late General Stewart of Garth, in his " Sketches of the Highlanders," relates a very remarkable instance of Second Sight which happened in his own family:—" Late on an autumn evening in the year 1773, the son of a neighbouring gentleman came to my father's house. He and my mother were from home; but several friends were in the house. The young gentleman spoke little, and seemed absorbed in deep thought. Soon after he arrived, he inquired for a boy of the family, then three years of age. When shown into the nursery, the nurse was trying on a pair of new shoes, and complained that they did not fit the child. ' They will fit him before he will have occasion for them,' said the young gentleman. This called forth the chidings of the nurse for predicting evil to the child, who was stout and healthy! When he returned to the party he had left in the sitting-room, who had heard of his observation on the shoes, they cautioned him to take care that the nurse did not derange his new talent of the second-sight, with some ironical congratulations on his pretended acquirement. This brought on an explanation, when he told them that as he had approached the end of a wooden bridge near the house, he was astonished to see a crowd of people passing the bridge. Coming nearer, he observed a person carrying a small coffin, followed by about twenty gentlemen, all of his acquaintance, his own father and mine being of the number, with a concourse of the country people. He did not attempt to join, but saw them turn off to the right, in the direction of the churchyard, which they entered. He then proceeded on his intended visit, much impressed with what he had seen, with a feeling of awe, and believing it to have been a representation of the death and funeral of a child of the family. The whole received perfect confirmation in his mind, by the sudden death of the boy the following night, and the consequent funeral, which was exactly as he had seen. This gentleman was not a professed seer. This was his first and his last vision. and, as he told me," says General Stewart, " it was sufficient."

A prophecy of war

Some forty years ago, there lived at Newton Moss, near Wick, an old woman called Mórag Guinne (Sarah Gunn). Her appearance was not prepossessing: she had a wrinkled face like tough leather, small piercing eyes, a hooked nose, and grey hair falling over her bony shoulders and sprouting from her pointed chin. She was known to be a " taibhsear," and was reputed to be a witch also. She used to sit on a three-legged stool inside her cottage and draw cabalistic designs with her broom-handle on the flagstones, from which she prophesied (for a monetary consideration) " the shape of things to come." Her " fios nam fàdh " (foreknowledge) seemed to be confined to dark and terrible happenings; and few who visited her cottage at dead of night to consult her, dared speak of what they had heard within its walls.

On one occasion, two anglers who happened to pass her cottage at dusk decided to ask for a cup of tea. The atmosphere inside the cottage was anything but friendly. After much haggling, the old woman agreed to make tea for them; but as she made it she muttered to herself in sinister monotones about trials and tribulations which would come upon the countryside. This got on the nerves of one of the anglers, who tried to divert the old woman's attention by some jocular remark. Disregard of her prophecies angered her, however, and drawing herself up she cursed him. " Ruith nah-Aoin' ort, deire nan seachd Sathurn' ort, agus na meal thusa do shlainte! " she shrieked (" The hurry of Friday be on you, the end of the seven Saturdays be upon you, and may you not enjoy your health!), and then went on to say, " I am an old woman, and near to death. Before I die, in one month's time, there will be increasing disquietude on the earth; and twenty years from now there will be mourning in my land, when many coffins will be borne eastward to the burying-ground in solemn procession. I ' see ' many a funeral, at the rate of five or more a day, of victims washed up on yonder shore! "

In about a month's time, Sarah Gunn died; and twenty years later (1940) the Second World War started, and, just as she had foretold, corpses were being daily washed ashore from vessels wrecked off the Caithness coast.

The death of the Duke of Sutherland

In 1892, the Duke and Duchess of Sutherland were not at the Northern Meeting Games at Inverness on the first day; but as nothing was known to be wrong, were expected from Dunrobin Castle on the second.

There was in the town a young police officer who saw " sealladh " (visions). On the night of the first day of the Games, this man dreamt that he was at the Gathering, and that while there he was handed a telegram to the effect that the Duke had died at 10.30 p.m. the night before. He woke trembling and related his dream to his family, who were more annoyed than credulous

As the policeman was trying to compose himself again, the telephone rang. It was the Chief Constable of Inverness—with the news that the Duke of Sutherland had died the previous evening at 10.30 o'clock.

A dead man shot by an arrow

Martin, the historian of the Western Isles, records the following instance of Second Sight, as related to him by Sir Norman MacLeod of Berneray:—

There was a man in Harris who was always being seen by those with Second Sight with an arrow in his thigh, and the islanders believed he would meet his death by being shot in some conflict. In course of time, however, the man died a natural death.

His body was brought up for burial to St. Clement's Church, at Rodil; and at the same time another funeral party arrived, with another body to be buried in the same church. An argument arose as to which party should enter the church first. A general melée followed, and someone let fly several arrows.

When Sir Norman MacLeod of Berneray, who was present, at last succeeded in persuading them to stop, it was discovered that an arrow had pierced the thigh of the dead man as he lay on the bier, waiting for burial. Thus were the Seer's predictions fulfilled.

Donald Black and "The Terror"

A man of the village of Caolas, in Tiree, Domhnull Mac an Duibh (Donald Black) was married for the fourth time. His corn was being kiln-dried and he was sitting up one night in the solitary hut where the kiln was kept, blowing on the fire to keep it alive, when the figure of his first wife appeared, and told him to beware, for " ant-eagal " (The Terror) was coming; it was at " crudhan eich " (The Horseshoe)—a landmark on the public road to Caolas, about a mile and a half away.

The heat of the fire made him drowsy, and Donald was dozing off to sleep when the figure of his second wife appeared, crying that The Terror was drawing near; it was at " Cachlaidh na Cuil Connaidh " (Gateway of the Fuel Enclosure). Disregarding this warning also, he was once more dropping off to sleep when another apparition appeared before him. This was his third wife, who said that The Terror was now at " Bail uachdrach " (the upper village).

This warning struck home, and Donald left the kiln with all speed and made for his cottage. He had hardly got into bed when the whole house was shaken as if by an earthquake. A violent wind-storm, the like of which had never before been known in Tiree, swept past the windows, carrying garden palings and all before it. The gale raged all night, but the house stood firm and its occupants were unharmed.

Funeral customs and the omens of death

Three knocks at regular intervals of one or two minutes might be heard in any part of the dwelling-house, on the entrance door, on a table, on a window, or even on the top of a " bun-bed." The sound was quite different from any other—dull and heavy— something eerie about them. A similar omen was the " dead-drap." Its sound resembled that of a continued drop of water falling slowly and regularly from a height; but it was leaden and hollow. Night was the usual time when they were heard. They were audible first by one person, and could not be heard by a second without taking hold of the one that first heard them. This was the case with all the sights and sounds that prognosticated death, and lasted for any length of time. Phenomena like these were universally admitted in the Highlands and Islands of Scotland.

Before the death of a member of the household, there was at times heard during the hours of darkness, the noise as if something heavy were being laid down outside the door of the dwelling-house—the noise of the coffin outside, before it was taken inside the house. A murmur of many voices was occasionally overheard about the front door—the harbinger of the conversation of those who were to assemble for the funeral.

The death lights

From the croft of Dunie near Kirkmichael two lights were observed (like candle lanterns) coming from a lonely cottage on the hillside one cold November night. The farmer and his three daughters clearly saw these two lights proceeding down the narrow winding brae-side pathway in the direction of the main road to Blairgowrie, when the mysterious lights suddenly disappeared. The farmer and his daughters thought the matter rather strange, but thought no more about it until about a fortnight afterwards two children developed diphtheria and died inside the same cottage. It was down the very same rough zig-zag path that the coffins containing both the bodies were carried on their way to the Kirkmichael churchyard.

The engines

The late Angus Morrison, who lived in a lonely cottage at Sheigra, near Cape Wrath, almost sixty miles from the nearest railway station, was an old sailor-fisherman. He wore one gold earring—after the old custom in certain districts in the North of Scotland—to help to pay for the cost of burial, should the wearer be drowned at sea and his body washed ashore.

Some twenty years ago, Angus Morrison told his friends how he frequently heard the noise of engines running at the top of a certain hill above his croft. He was insistent, despite their scepticism, and asserted that he often heard the sound at night as well as through the day. There was no road to the place indicated, far less a railway line. During the Second World War, a radar station was set up on the exact spot he had indicated. He had only heard the sound of its engines a few years in advance

The spirit multitude

The West Wind was believed to bring in its train the "sluagh" (spirit multitude) which descended on the Western Highlands and the Hebrides from time to time. Few have seen the spirit host that follows in the wake of the West Wind; but on clear frosty nights many have heard their conflicts in the sky—the shouting of the combatants and the clashing of their armour.

The "sluagh" was believed to consist of the spirits of men, and it was said to hover over the places where the individuals composing it had transgressed when in human form. This aerial army might easily invade a dwelling house unobserved, though every precaution was taken against them. They often come down to earth; and when the night is dark and the sea roars with anger on the rocks, the people of Barra and South Uist declare that the "sluagh" is seeking shelter in the grasses by the shore; and queer tales are still told in Benbecula of human beings carried off by the spirit host.

Wild swans

Wild swans are called in the North "the enchanted sons of kings." They swim in the shape of white birds on the waterways and fly across the northern sky; and are believed to lament as they go:—

"There is nothing anywhere for us now but brown earth and drifting clouds and wan waters. Why should we not go from place to place as the wind goes, and see each day new fields of reeds, new forest trees, new mountains? Oh, we shall never see the star-heart of any mountain again!"

It is said that the watcher by the shores of the firth or by the lonely mountain tarn may see the wild swans taking off their "cochull" (coverings) and resuming their proper shape as men in their endeavours to free themselves from the spell they are under. This however is impossible until three times three hundred years have passed.

7

MISCELLANEOUS TALES

Smuggling in the Highlands

Illicit distilling has been practically suppressed in the North of Scotland, and with the exception of a few very remote places, smuggling is extinct. Smuggling stories, however, with their glamour and romance, will always be a part of Scottish folklore and literature.

Like other important inventions and discoveries, the origin of distillation is shrouded in doubt and uncertainty; but according to one writer, it is ascribed to Osiris, the great god, and, perhaps, the first King of Egypt, who is said to have taught his people various arts and sciences. According to another, the art of separating alcohol from fermented liquors, which appears to have been known in the far East from the most remote antiquity, is supposed to have been practised by the Chinese, whence the knowledge of distilling the water of life—as *aqua vitae* or "*uisge-beatha*"—travelled westward. Adam, of course, who spoke the Gaelic, had engaged in smuggling outside the walls of Eden, and plucky Maclean, who sailed a boat of his own at the Flood, had an anker of good old Highland whisky on board.

Lure of the Pipes

As told to me by a native of the district

The scene was the heart of Diebidale deer forest in Ross-shire, the time was nearing midnight in the late December long ago, when the " Wee People " danced on the top of the bogs that even a wild duck could not cross without breaking the surface. Halfway up one of the hills, known as Corrie Glas, stood Big John Clach-na-Harnich, and beside him were his two famous black dogs—a dog and a bitch. Big John was the head stalker on Diebidale, and he had been out all day and most of the night after the hinds, which they were shooting off. It had turned out to be a wild night, with a half moon; and John had taken shelter for a while against the buffettings of the storm.

At last the night cleared a bit and he started for home. As it was late, he decided to go round the side of the hill and take a short cut home. He had been that road often before, and knew every step of it, and he could also jump the Poacher's Pool at Allt a'choin (The Dog's Burn) and still cut a few more miles off his road.

If there was one thing on earth Big John loved besides good whisky, it was the pipes, and as he came near Allt a'choin, he thought he heard bagpipe music. He stopped and listened, and sure enough, there it was, away to his right; and that piper could play! He was playing " Braham Castle," and John never heard it played so well before. He could not resist the music and started to walk towards it. He wondered as he went along who the piper could be, and what possessed him to come there and play on a night like that. As he neared the place where the sounds came from, the moon went behind the clouds and it became very dark.

Things seemed to become very still as he walked on, and the sound of the pipes grew louder. The piper was now playing a reel—the finest reel John ever heard; and through the music he thought he heard hooching. All of'a sudden, he saw a light, and going nearer, he saw a fail-roofed house. John knew he was not very far by now from the Poacher's Pool and Rory-the-Glen's " Black bothy "; but he could not remember ever seeing this place before. The sound of the pipes drew him on however, and he went forward to the door. But here a queer thing happened—the black bitch which would tackle the biggest stag in Diebidale, would not go another step. John stopped, and tried to coax her on, but she would not move, and lay down. Then John remembered that a bitch would not follow her master if the Unknown was in front. He was shaken at this; but the lure of the pipes was too great, and he said, " Very well, you can stay here; as long as I have Black Simon with me and Killsure (his gun) under my arm, I'll face anything."

The piper was now playing " Tulloch Gorm," and what a piper—the time he kept! Just as John went up to the door, it opened, and an old woman said—" Come in John, I'm sure you will be near starved to death with the cold." John thanked her, and said he would come in for a minute or two and hear the pipes. As he entered the house he took off his bonnet, and the old woman made to take it from him; but Black Simon, snarling and growling, snatched the bonnet out of his hand and held it in his mouth. The old woman then opened the kitchen door; and the sight that met John, he'll never forget. The house was full of men and girls. They were the finest looking girls he had ever seen. They were nearly all dressed the same, in long frocks of a queer bluish-red colour; the men had greenish-red clothes. John had ears only for the piper however; and he looked round to see where he was.

There he stood, near to the bed-closet door, and behind the spinning wheel to give room to the dancers. John was stunned when he saw the piper. Of all the pipers he had ever seen or heard about, this one was the King. He had on the full Highland dress; but for the life of him John could not tell the tartan. And the pipes! what pipes!—solid gold mounted—and as he played the Reel-o'-Tulloch, John thought he could see the blue sparks flying from his fingers and smoke coming from the chanter.

The music stopped, and the piper looked at John and smiled; but never spoke.

The only one that spoke of the whole company was the old woman, who then asked John if he would take a dram. He said he would, and she gave him a glass of good stuff. If the music was good, the whisky was better. As soon as he took the first sip, he thought his whole body was on fire right to the soles of his feet.

John drained the glass, and then the piper started to play again—a schottishe this time—and the best-looking of the girls came towards John holding out her hands, smiling at him and silently inviting him to dance. The whisky had done its work well; and John thought he could manage the dance fine, and was on the point of taking the girl in his arms, when Black Simon again jumped in front of him. John looked down at the dog, wondering what was wrong with him, and then he saw, peeping from below the girl's long frock, instead of dainty feet, two horses' hooves. He drew back frightened out of his wits; and then looking towards the closet door where the piper stood, he saw a long red streak coming oozing out from below the door. He knew then the company he was in, and also that his end was near, and shouted " God help me! " He could not have chosen better words; for all at once he saw the faces change, the piper's tartan turned to red, and over the blow-stock of the pipes, from which smoke and sparks emanated, he saw the face of Lucifer himself grinning at him.

He took his only chance, and with one bound, reached the door and turned to call Black Simon, who had twice that night saved him, and was doing it a third time—for as John sprang for the door, the dog sprang at Nick; and as John turned, he saw Old Horny draw the dirk from its sheath (still wet with the blood of its last victim) and raise it to kill Black Simon.

Quick as a flash, John's up with " Killsure " and let drive with both barrels; but that was all the good it did, for John, who was hardly ever known to miss, saw the lead splash on the wall behind, after going harmlessly through Old Nick.

John then bolted, and ran as hard as he could for the Poacher's Pool; but fast as he was, he found he was no match for the one who followed. Looking back, he saw the Monster, and on each side of him two of the girls, now howling fiends, with flames of fire streaming from their heads in place of the fair hair they had earlier. He could hear the clatter of their horses' hooves as they raced over the rocks and heather.

John heard the gurgle of the water of the Poacher's Pool, and made a last supreme effort to reach it. Better to die in the cool water among the salmon, he thought, than be torn to bits by fingers of fire.

Then just as Old Nick raised his bloody dirk to strike, across the water at Rory-the-Glen's a cock crew in the morning. John fell unconscious on the brink of the Pool, and it was hours after when he came to, to find his two dogs licking his face. " Oh," said he, " Black Simon, I thought that your end came as the dirk fell "; but then Black Simon rolled over on his back, and John saw on the dog's breast four white hairs, and he knew that the Devil was powerless against the black dog as long as he had those hairs.

And so to this day, if you listen at the Poacher's Pool, you will hear in the running water the sound of the pipes, on nights when the "Wee People" dance on the bogs, and the wind blows round Corrie Glas.

Crunar the cruel

About the year 1625, there was born at Kingellie in the parish of Kirkhill, near Inverness, a strong, robust, overbearing, and cruel individual called " Crunar Fraser." He was endowed with more than an ordinary portion of physical strength which in these bygone days was considered of very great importance. Crunar Fraser carried his cruelty to such excess, however, that he became the terror of the country. His Chief saw in him the makings of a good soldier and got him a commission in the army. Shortly afterwards, he was sent to Ireland, where civil war had broken out. His stepmother, inwardly rejoicing at getting rid of such a wild character, accompanied him to Inverness and on coming to the bridge, she told him she intended going no further. Before bidding him farewell, however, she put a charm around his neck which she said would guard him against steel and bullet. " And how long will the charm last? " asked Crunar. " Until you see my face again," his stepmother replied. Believing that if he destroyed his stepmother on the spot the charm would remain with him all his days, he unsheathed his sword and with one mighty swoop, severed her head from her body.

On his arrival in Ireland, he joined his regiment, and it was not long before his courage, daring and skill placed him in an unequalled position. As an officer, he exercised his powers mercilessly towards all those of his enemies who were unfortunate enough to fall within his cruel grasp. No quarter was given to any who fell into his clutches. It is said that on one occasion when a beautiful young girl arrested for a moment his murderous arm as he was on the point of thrusting his sword through her husband, he stayed his hand only for a second, and then cruelly murdered her husband who was a gallant and brave officer. The lady was spared but only for the purpose of

carrying her off to the Highlands as his bride. As he was returning from the field with the lady seated on horseback behind him,
he felt the fair lady's hands on his dirk. He instantly killed her
and threw her lifeless body into the stream over which he
happened then to be passing.

Meanwhile at home, news of Crunar's warlike exploits
spread throughout the country, and although there were many
of his clan who were proud of him and lauded these exploits,
there were also a great number who dreaded his return. Strangely
enough, after his return to the Highlands, he settled down to
the life of a quiet and peaceful farmer, much to the surprise of
the inhabitants of the district who expected him to return a
ferocious and bloody soldier.

Some time before his death a company of Irish soldiers
stationed in Inverness, on learning that Crunar still lived, and
that his abode was within seven miles of the town, decided to
put an end to his existence and avenge the havoc he committed
among their own people in Ireland. Crunar, who was warned
of their intention, requested those around him to carry him
out to the east end of his house in order that he could meet his
enemies in the open. Crunar was only just able to raise himself
on his elbow as he saw the Irish soldiers approaching about a
quarter of a mile away. Filling his lungs to their full extent he
gave a tremendous roar which re-echoed among the surrounding
hills. Hastily the Irish soldiers retraced their steps, being of the
opinion that Crunar was still a desperate and bloodthirsty warrior
instead of a bed-ridden invalid.

Never again was Crunar Fraser interfered with and he died
in peace at a ripe old age. Local legend has it that ever afterwards
the house of Crunar Fraser was haunted. It has long since
crumbled into ruins, and not a vestige of it remains.

The Black Officer of Ballachroan

About the year 1700, the old farmhouse of Ballachroan near
Kingussie was the home of a certain Captain John Macpherson—
known as the " Black Officer." Captain Macpherson, a zealous

recruiting officer, was also believed by many people of the district at that time, to be an agent of the devil and belief was strengthened on account of an incident in the lonely bothy of Gaick.

The " Black Officer," a keen sportsman, had invited a number of people to join him in a hunting expedition to Gaick on Christmas Day. The place of meeting was arranged to be the house of the " Post Ban " near Aultlarie, but when the appointed time for the meeting arrived, none appeared but the " Post Ban " who was a letter carrier and consequently a dependant of the " Black Officer." When the Captain arrived and saw that none of his guests had turned up, he was very annoyed, but the " Post Ban " meekly suggested postponing the expedition until the following day. The Captain swore and said that he would not postpone it as he had an appointment to be in Gaick that night.

There was no help for it, the two huntsmen set off taking with them their guns, two dogs, and some provisions, and arrived at the bothy very late that night. A good fire was soon kindled and a meal prepared, but during all this time the Captain was restless and kept on drinking a large quantity of whisky. Towards midnight, the dogs became restless also and began to growl and so the Captain tied them to the bedpost and ordered the " Post Ban " to go to sleep. The " Post " complied by wrapping himself in his plaid and stretching himself on his heather bed, but the " Black Officer " continued his restless pacing to and fro. Suddenly a knock sounded at the door and the Captain immediately started trembling and the dogs strained at the leash and growled fiercely. The " Post Ban " sprang from his bed and made to open the door, but the Captain waved him back and told him he would open the door himself. As the door was opened the " Post Ban " caught sight of a tall dark figure but was unable to see whether the caller was man or woman. The Captain went out quickly, closing the door behind him and the " Post Ban " set himself to listen but all he could hear was the murmur of angry voices and when the caller was leaving, the " Post Ban " heard the Captain say that he would be at the same spot a year from that night and that he would bring a number of persons with him. When the Captain re-entered the bothy he was pale and trembling and made straight for the whisky flask from which he took a good pull before telling the " Post Ban " that his late visitor was a gentleman he had invited to hunt, who was disappointed that the guests did not turn up, and went home. The " Post Ban " asked the Captain if the visitor had far to go and was informed that he had a fair distance but that he had a fleet horse which would soon take him home.

When daylight came the " Post Ban " examined the ground for the marks of the horse's hoofs, but failed to find any. On arriving home he told his wife and friends of what he saw and heard and all who heard his story were convinced that the " Black Officer " was under the influence of the devil.

A year passed, and as Christmas was once more drawing near it became known that Captain Macpherson intended to arrange another hunting expedition to Gaick. Many of the people who had been invited the previous year temporarily left the country, while others feigned illness. The " Post Ban," however, had an adventurous son who rejected the warnings of his father and mother and joined the hunting party. This son was said to be under the evil spell of the " Black Officer."

The " Black Officer " left Ballachroan for Gaick the evening before Christmas with four companions and some dogs. The " Post Ban's " son and a few more of the party were to follow later. As the " Post Ban's " son and his followers approached Buidebeg both sides of Ban's brogues came away from the uppers leaving him bare-footed, and consequently it was impossible for young Ban to go any further, and his followers, at once giving way to superstitious fear, decided to abandon the journey also. In the meantime, the " Black Officer " and his party were well on the way to Gaick. That night a fearful storm swept over Badenoch and continued throughout the following day. The relatives of the " Black Officer's " companions began to get very anxious for their safety, and fear began to spread throughout the countryside when it became generally known what the " Post Ban " had experienced the previous year. Various methods were tried to ascertain the fate of the hunting party but without result until at last someone devised the following superstitious method of obtaining the information. The youngest member of the family was placed on what was called a " goggan " and then questioned for the information required. The powers of the child were supposed to be governed by some supernatural power and the answers were firmly believed by the people.

The following day a search party headed by an old soldier was organised and proceeded to Gaick. On reaching the bothy at Gaick the search party found it to be in ruins, the greater part of it having been swept away. On entering the bothy they found two bodies lying stiff on the bed, while on the floor was another in a crouching position with one stocking on and the other clasped in his hand. Near the door lay the body of Captain Macpherson and behind him lay the carcases of the dogs and the bodies of three others belonging to the party. This accounted for all but one of the " Black Officer's " party and after a further search the body was found lying face downwards at some considerable distance from the bothy. The bodies were then placed on crude stretchers and the search party then proceeded homewards carrying the remains. They had not gone far, however, when a violent storm arose, compelling them to take shelter. The old soldier leading them told them to place the body of the " Black Officer " behind, and when this was done the storm suddenly ceased and the procession carried on home.

The brewer of Glen Affric

There passed away, some years ago in Strathglass, at the age of ninety, John Fraser, more widely known by the suggestive *alias* of " The Brewer." In his early days John had been a noted smuggler, and many a good story he would tell over a dram. Although his trade was brewing, it was well known that he distilled on the sly.

John was also a keen fisher and poacher, and was frequently to be found innocently casting away on the river banks; but the eye of the Excise was continuously fastened upon his movements. He was generally successful in cheating the officers on his track.

On one occasion John was coming down the glen with a disguised " anker " on his back and his rod in his hand, when he recognised the well-known form of the exciseman in the distance. He ran to the river, put up his fishing-rod and carefully consigned his cask to the stream, which was in flood at the time. Making sure that the gauger saw him innocently fishing for a few minutes, he climbed up the bank on to the main road, and hurried on.

With solemn face he was passing the exciseman when the latter enquired: " Where now, John, will you be going to fish in such a hurry? " " Oh, the fish are not taking," said John. " I'm really going to Beauly for a doctor; my wife is very ill." John passed on, followed by the sympathy of the exciseman.

Continuing his journey till the gauger was out of sight, John then sent down to the river and found the little barrel intact sailing down the flood to meet him!

From a box in his hut in Glen Affric, John was always able to produce a good glass of the finest " brew."

The legend of Puill Dubha Ghaunn

As told to me by a native of the district

There is, I understand, more than one version of the legend of Puill Dubha Ghaunn; but I received the following narrative, a few years ago from a local authority.

A long while ago, a Swedish Prince set sail from his home country in order to collect bullion due to him from certain of the Orkney and Shetland islanders as also from some Lewismen. In his ship were coffers containing money for the sailors' wages for manning the boats, and altogether a lot of hard cash was involved.

The Prince gathered his money from the Shetland Islands first of all, and left some of his stores and sailing gear behind at Lerwick, intending to pick these up later on, on his return voyage to Sweden.

After he had abstracted funds from Orkney, he put into port in the Island of Lewis in order to continue his collection of shekels there, and by the time he had completed his business, he had stored up a considerable cargo of gold on board his ship. Before leaving Stornoway, a witch (" Seer ") boarded the boat and warned him to beware of the following three places: Sgeirin Bhaorach Hulm (the beastly sharp rocks off Holm); Creagan Grat an-Fhoruna (the dangerous rocks off Cape Wrath); and Puill Dubha Ghaunn (the black pools of Ghaunn) near Kylestrome. After leaving Stornoway, on his homeward voyage to Sweden, a favourable southerly breeze sprang up; but while rounding the Butt of Lewis, the wind suddenly changed to the north-west, when a terrible hurricane ripped a waymost of the sails and rigging, and the Swedish vessel was forced to run into Puill Dubha Ghaunn for shelter.

Now, it so happened that MacLeod of Ardvreck Castle (the then Laird of Assynt) was somewhat financially embarrassed, and when news reached him that a Swedish boat had anchored in Puill Dubha Ghaunn with some notable people and plenty of money on board—money which he presumed had been collected out of certain rents from Orkney and Shetland and the Outer Hebrides—he forthwith assembled his retainers and marched for Kylesku, headed by his piper and with his " fool " by his side. All great men in these days had a " fool " to entertain them, and to act as gillie. That fool's name was Clark and he accompanied his master everywhere he went. On arrival at Kylesku Ferry, MacLeod's party launched all the available boats they could gather, and made straight for Puill Dubha Ghaunn As they approached the Prince's vessel, all the boats dispersed as if they were preparing for the fishing; but the one with MacLeod, his piper, and his fool and a few of his retainers on board, made straight for the Swedish ship. On getting to within shouting distance, they were challenged by the Prince's crew to ascertain whether they had come for peace or war. Instantly MacLeod took off his bonnet (a token in these days of peace), unbuckled his scabbard and placed his bonnet over the point of his claymore as a symbol of peace and respect to the Prince, as was the customary way of paying homage to great people from overseas who landed on Scottish territory.

As MacLeod and his men were boarding the Swedish ship, his piper struck up " MacLeod's Salute," which caused great pleasure to the Prince and his sailors, and once on deck, they were treated with the greatest of hospitality.

The piper played for a time to the Prince and then went below to the crew's quarters, where graybeards of all sorts were freely opened and drained to the dregs. While MacLeod and the Prince were enjoying each other's company on very friendly terms, MacLeod took great pains to show off his bonnet with his crest and its three eagle's feathers, and to explain the meaning of these things.

At a given signal (from MacLeod) the fool drew his dirk and stabbed the Prince from behind in the region of the heart—killing him instantly.

With all the gaiety going on and the noise of the pipes, nobody but the fool, MacLeod and one or two of his closest friends suspected anything unusual had happened until an armed retinue of MacLeod's men mounted guard over the crew's quarters. During the time all this was taking place, two or three of MacLeod's followers went ashore and procured the hides of two bullocks. When they rowed back to the ship with them, they concealed as much of the gold from the Swedish chests inside the bullock skins as they could hold.

The orgy continued until darkness set in, by which time drinking was at its height and graybeards filled up again and again, and handed round the whole crew.

After all was set and ready, MacLeod and his supporters rowed ashore, where they buried the treasure inside a cairn on the shore of Loch Cairnbawn in the darkness of the night.

When they returned to collect the gold a few days later, they had forgotten the exact spot where they had concealed it and were unable to find the cairn.

After a long and tedious search, three of MacLeod's best friends started to quarrel, and from words came blows, and blows gave way to swords. Two of the three men were slain outright and the third died two days later from his wounds, and the fool fell from his boat the same evening and was drowned in Loch Cairnbawn. So the treasure was never found.

When the crew of the Swedish ship awakened from their drunken slumbers, they were horrified to find the dead body of their master, and the treasure gone.

So they thereupon disembowelled their master's body and embalmed his carcass in salt and buried his entrails (which they also embalmed) in a grave by a small grassy plot of ground, near a rowan tree, on an eminence on the rocky shore of Loch Cairnbawn. Thereafter, they set sail for Sweden as fast as possible, taking their Prince's remains with them.

And so the witch's prediction concerning Puill Dubha Ghaunn came true. A raven is said to guard the cairn in which the accursed gold is hidden; but woe betide anyone who should attempt to remove the riches.

Iain Beag MacAindra

Little John MacAndrew

The story of Iain Beag MacAindra, the gallant little archer of Strathspey, is fairly well known. The main purpose here is to give the Gaelic words attributed to Mackintosh of Kyllachy.

Iain Beag MacAindra's home was at Dalnahaitnach on the banks of the Dulnan a few miles above Carr Bridge. He had attained so much skill with the bow and arrow that his fame was known far and wide and on this account he was treated with due respect. Very small he was in stature, but in courage and resource he was great.

While Iain Beag was on a visit to Strathdearn the Laird of Auchluachrach, attended by a body of his clansmen, was on his way home with cattle he had raided from the lands of Rose of Kilravock in Nairnshire. The raiders were looking forward to reaching home in safety with their booty but at Cro-clach in Strathdearn they were overtaken by Rose of Kilravock and MacKintosh of Kyllachy with a band of their own followers. Kyllachy, being aware of Iain Beag MacAindra's skill with the bow and arrow, asked him to join them in attacking the raiders. Iain Beag agreed and in the fierce fight which followed he gave a good account of himself. The chief of the raiders was killed by an arrow directed by the unerring aim of the gallant little archer, When Kyllachy saw that the raiders' leader had fallen he shouted. " Tapa leat fhéin, Iain Beag MacAindra bho Dalnahaitnach, 'se do laimh rinn sud." (Thanks to yourself, little John MacAndrew from Dalnahaitnach, it was your hand that did that.) Iain Beag however, instantly suspected the design underlying Kyllachy's wily words and he gave the angry retort, " Mile mallachd air do theanga Iain h Yallachy, is eagal ort." (A thousand curses on your tongue, John of Kyllachy and you afraid.) Kyllachy knew that the enemy would seek revenge for the death of their leader and his purpose, therefore, was to direct the attention of the enemy to Iain Beag MacAindra at Dalnahaitnach thus hoping that Strathdearn would escape further trouble from them. All the raiders were killed except a boy placed at some distance as a scout. The boy hastened home and told the tragic tale.

Iain Beag returned to his home at Dalnahaitnach convinced that Auchluachrach's men were bent on revenge and would seek him out. He at once took precautionary measures. He improvised a place of refuge for himself in a great tree near the door of his house. In this hiding place he placed his bow and arrows. One day he saw some strangers in the wood at some distance from his house. He immediately guessed their errand, but they, on their part, did not imagine that the insignificant looking little fellow was the man they were after. They spoke him fair and asked if he would direct them to the house of Iain Beag MacAindra. He complied and together they reached the house. They entered. Telepathy passed between Iain Beag and his wife. She entertained the strangers with food and drink while her husband sat meekly by the fire. Suddenly she cuffed his ears and ordered him out to see if the master of the house was coming. He grumbled but obeyed.

Once outside he climbed into his place of ambush in the tree and got his trusty bow and arrows ready. His wife then told the strangers that the master of the house had arrived and was outside. Out they went on mischief intent but one by one they were killed by the arrows of the skilful archer from his perch in the tree. He spared the last man, however, and to him he said, " Dhachaidh's innis do naigheachd."(Go home and tell your tale.)

It is not recorded that Auchluachrach's men made any further attempts on the life of Iain Beag MacAindra. A monument to the little but redoubtable archer can still be seen near the roadside at Dalnahaitnach farm.

The Tales